NEVADA GROWN

A YEAR IN LOCAL FOOD

NEVADA GROWN

A YEAR IN LOCAL FOOD

BAOBAB PRESS
RENO, NEVADA

Copyright © 2015 NevadaGrown

First Edition
15 16 17   10 9 8 7 6 5 4 3 2 1

ISBN-13: 978-1-936097-12-8
ISBN-10: 1-936097-12-5

Library of Congress Control Number: 2015953267

Baobab Press
121 California Avenue
Reno, Nevada 89509
www.baobabpress.com

Cover Design by Travis Bennett

Printed in China.

CONTENTS

I remember vividly the jaw-dropping comment from a Nevada farmer that propelled my journey into local food. It was August 2004, and I was market manager for the state's largest farmers market in Sparks. After decades of eating bland grocery store food, I found myself surrounded by local farms and nostalgic tastes from childhood: fresh corn, juicy tomatoes, and melons and berries so sweet they tasted like candy, all grown in Nevada.

On the last farmers market of the season, I stopped by a Nevada farmer's booth and asked where I could buy her produce now that market season was over. Her reply is etched forever in my memory. "Nowhere," she replied. "You can't buy from us again until farmers markets start up next year."

She said they would be tilling everything back into the soil and that local farms had few places to sell their produce. Grocery stores and restaurants rarely bought local produce because they preferred the convenience of distributors and large agribusiness growers.

I didn't sleep that night, thinking about the tons of fabulous local food being tilled back into the soil and the family farms struggling to make a living.

What has changed since that August night in 2004? Across Nevada and across America, more people, just like me, began to rediscover the joys of local food that had been buried and almost forgotten with the advent of industrial agriculture and the resulting changes in our food system.

Nevada Grown: A Year in Local Food is a celebration of Nevada's thriving food culture and an invitation to discover the diverse and bountiful harvest Nevada's hardworking and talented farmers and ranchers deliver.

Be adventurous and try the recipes in this cookbook. They range from simple to complicated, health conscious to indulgent, newly concocted to generational, and eclectic to traditional. Source your ingredients from local farms and ranches, and discover that turnips and beets are delicious when they're young, tender, and fresh from the field. Rediscover the taste of beef and pork raised on local ranches. Relish the flavor and freshness of locally produced eggs and honey. Be brave and add kohlrabi, sunchokes, and fennel to your farmers market list.

Enjoy the recipes, enjoy the stories behind every recipe, and most of all, enjoy the journey.

Ann Louhela, Co-Editor
President, NevadaGrown

As I write these words in early fall 2015 — with pumpkins in their patches in Northern Nevada and sweet succulent carrots flourishing down south and the honey flow from across the state already bottled — I remember that chilly day in spring 2013 when Ann Louhela approached me about a partnership.

Would I be interested, she asked, in helping to showcase Nevada produce, meat and other products and to let people know how and where to buy them? Of course I would.

Through her work with farmers markets, NevadaGrown (which promotes Nevada agriculture), and the Western Nevada College Specialty Crop Institute, Ann had become a leading advocate for local food. And one of my joys and privileges as the food and drink editor of RGJ Media is telling people about the bounty that surrounds them in the Silver State.

Our talk eventually became "Home Means Delicious," a play on the official state song, "Home Means Nevada." The weekly column ran in the *Reno Gazette-Journal* newspaper and on RGJ.com; it featured a seasonal local ingredient and a recipe for using the ingredient. Many recipes were submitted by farmers and readers.

Nevada Grown: A Year in Local Food is the culmination of "Home Means Delicious." I'm listed as the co-editor of the cookbook, but with this project, I was at least as much student as editor.

From Ann Louhela and Nevada's farmers, I learned about how crops are grown and livestock are raised, about the economics of farming and the ways farmers can connect with new markets. The folks who submitted recipes reminded me that eating local isn't a mere slogan — it's something we can incorporate into the ways and dishes we already cook at home.

But the most important lesson was this: without customers, farmers (especially small family farmers) cannot stay in business. My wish is that *Nevada Grown: A Year in Local Food* helps farmers stay on the farm by inspiring you, wherever you live, to visit a farm stand or farmers market or food co-op and purchase local ingredients to prepare the recipes we're sharing.

Co-editing this cookbook ranks among the greatest pleasures and purposes in my career as a food writer. I hope you take from it some of this pleasure and purpose.

Johnathan L. Wright, Co-Editor
Food and Drink Editor, RGJ Media

SPRING

LEMON VERBENA MINT HERB TEA
Diane Greene, Herbs by Diane

½ cup fresh mint leaves (not the stems, as they're bitter), rinsed, lightly packed (about 20 leaves)

½ cup fresh lemon verbena leaves, rinsed, lightly packed (about 10 to 15 leaves)

2 cups of water

Bring water almost but not quite to a boil. Put the mint and verbena leaves in a teapot. Pour hot water over the leaves and steep for 3 to 5 minutes. Strain into tea cups. Makes 2 cups.

• • •

SORREL PESTO
Janet Knight, L.O.V.E. On Your Plate

2 cups fresh sorrel, ribs removed, coarsely chopped

⅓ cup packed fresh parsley leaves

2 garlic cloves, roughly chopped

⅓ cup freshly grated Parmesan cheese

¼ cup pine nuts

½ teaspoon salt

¼ cup olive oil

Note: Sorrel adds a tangy lemon flavor to the pesto. It is great with pasta or as a thick sauce for fish. Sorrel also makes a wonderful soup and is catching on with the juicing community.

In a food processor or blender, purée all ingredients until smooth. Store pesto in a jar with a tight-fitting lid and refrigerate. The refrigerated pesto will last for about two weeks. Makes about 1 cup.

BAKED KALE CHIPS

Amanda Gaffaney

---

1 bunch kale, not curly

1 tablespoon olive oil

1 teaspoon sea salt

Note: My little ones love these, and they're a healthy alternative to chips. Different types of kale will give different flavors, some milder than others. Dino kale, also known as Tuscan, is our favorite.

Preheat oven to 350 degrees. Line a non-insulated cookie sheet with parchment paper. With a knife or kitchen shears, carefully remove the leaves from the thick stems of the kale and tear into bite-size pieces. Wash and dry thoroughly with a salad spinner. Drizzle kale with olive oil and sprinkle with salt. Mix together and spread in a single layer on the cookie sheet. Bake until the edges are brown but not burned, 10 to 15 minutes. Check after 7 to 8 minutes.

ORANGE-SCENTED BEETS
Arianne Smith

---

4 cups beets, peeled and cubed	black pepper, to taste
1 tablespoon orange zest	1 teaspoon balsamic vinegar
1 tablespoon olive oil	½ teaspoon salt

Preheat oven to 375 degrees. Combine beets, orange zest, olive oil, and black pepper in a roasting pan. Toss well to coat. Bake for 45 minutes or until tender, stirring occasionally. Stir in vinegar and salt. Serves 6.

• • •

BROILED BEET SLICES
Sarah Smith

---

6 medium beets, scrubbed	1 tablespoon garlic, minced
½ cup water	1 tablespoon fresh ginger, finely grated
¼ cup butter	1 tablespoon soy sauce or tamari
2 tablespoons pure maple syrup	

Preheat oven to 400 degrees. Place beets in a small roasting pan with ½ cup water. Cover with foil and bake until beets are tender when pierced, about 45 to 60 minutes. Allow beets to cool slightly, then run under cool water and slip off the skins. Slice into rounds.

In a small pan, melt butter over medium heat. Stir in the maple syrup, garlic, ginger, and soy sauce or tamari. When ingredients are thoroughly combined, remove from heat.

Place the beets in a shallow baking pan and pour the maple syrup mixture over them. Broil, stirring occasionally until beets are caramelized, 5 to 10 minutes. Serves 4.

PICKLED BABY BEETS WITH HORSERADISH

Natalie Sellers, 4th Street Bistro

2 dozen baby beets, roasted and peeled

grated zest of one orange

¼ cup apple cider vinegar

½ cup red wine vinegar

¾ cup dry red wine

2 tablespoons fresh lemon juice

¼ cup white sugar

¼ cup brown sugar

2 teaspoons kosher or sea salt

8 whole allspice berries

15 whole cloves

¼ cup prepared horseradish

Note: Sierra Valley Farms baby beets and their fresh-ground organic horseradish in the jar are the inspirations for this recipe!

Place the cooked beets in a glass heatproof jar. In a stainless-steel pan, combine the remaining ingredients and bring to a boil. Immediately reduce the heat. Stir and simmer for 2 minutes until the sugar has dissolved.

Pour this mixture over the beets and cool to room temperature, uncovered. Cover and refrigerate. Will keep for about one month, refrigerated.

GREEN POTSTICKERS
Melody Poland

Dipping Sauce

½ cup balsamic vinegar

1 teaspoon raspberry jam

1 garlic clove, crushed

Potstickers

2 tablespoons olive oil

1 shallot, minced

6 cups fresh cooking greens
(mustard, beet, turnip)

½ teaspoon paprika

dash of salt

½ teaspoon black pepper

½ teaspoon mirin or sherry

½ cup crumbled goat cheese

¼ cup chopped cranberries (optional)

¼ cup chopped pine nuts (optional)

12-ounce package wonton wrappers

Dipping Sauce

Heat vinegar in a small saucepan with jam and crushed garlic over medium heat. Once the vinegar starts to boil, turn the heat down to low and allow it to simmer for a few more minutes or until it thickens. Strain crushed garlic from sauce and serve with the potstickers.

Potstickers

Heat olive oil in large frying pan over medium heat. Sauté shallots until light brown. Add greens, paprika, salt, pepper, and mirin or sherry, stirring until greens are wilted and some of the moisture has cooked out of the greens. Remove from heat and allow to cool.

Blend greens mixture in food processor or blender with goat cheese and optional pine nuts and chopped cranberries. Place wonton wrappers on a flat surface, and working quickly to prevent them from drying out, place a tablespoon of filling on to the center of each wrapper.

Wet edge of wrapper with a moistened fingertip and fold in half to seal. Crimp ends to keep filling contained. Heat a large frying pan over medium heat, and coat with the other tablespoon of olive oil.

Place potstickers in frying pan for one minute. Flip and fry the other sides for one minute. Add ¼ cup water to pan and cover. Steam potstickers for 4 minutes. When liquid evaporates, remove from heat and transfer to a plate. Serve warm. Makes 20 to 30.

AVOCADO & MICROGREEN SPRING ROLLS
WITH SPICY TAHINI DIPPING SAUCE
Avalon Korringa and Ryan Quantz, Urban Hydro Greens

Dipping Sauce	Spring Rolls
¼ cup tahini	2 avocados
¼ cup water	1 large cucumber
2 small cloves garlic	¼ head of red cabbage
1 small, marble-sized piece of ginger	2 to 3 carrots
2 tablespoons Bragg's Liquid Aminos or soy sauce	1 bunch cilantro
	1 bunch basil
1 tablespoon agave nectar	6 to 8 edible flowers
1 lime, juiced	1 ½ to 2 cups bok choy microgreens or your favorite variety
1 teaspoon red-pepper flakes	
	1 package (8 ½-inch) spring roll wrappers
	1 ounce cellophane noodles (bean threads)

Note: We designed these spring rolls to delight the senses! Your eyes are met with a colorful bouquet of edible flowers and vegetables delicately contained in a translucent rice-paper wrapper. Your mouth is met with an explosion of fresh vegetables, flavorful herbs, and microgreens. The array of flavors is accented by a delightful body of texture from snappy carrots to soft and slippery cellophane noodles. Everything about this dish is fresh and lovely and will leave you with a happy, healthy body and mind.

Dipping Sauce
Add all ingredients into a high-powered blender and blend until smooth, scraping down the sides of the blender as needed. Set aside until serving.

Spring Rolls

Bring one quart of water to a boil. Meanwhile, place the cellophane noodles in a medium-sized glass or ceramic mixing bowl. Pour boiling water over the noodles and cover with a large plate to keep the steam in. Steep noodles for at least 20 minutes.

While waiting, start to prep the veggies for the rolls.

Avocado: Cut in half, remove pit, scoop out the flesh, and cut into ¼-inch slices.
Cucumber: Cut in half lengthwise and scoop out seeds. Cut into thin slices.
Carrots: Cut into 3-inch sections, and then cut into matchsticks.
Red cabbage: Cut very thin to yield fine, long shreds.
Basil: Remove leaves from stems and cut into a fine chiffonade.
Cilantro: Pull off leaves, discard stems, and cut into a fine chiffonade.
Edible flowers: Gently pull petals from flowers and discard the center.
Microgreens: No preparation needed.

When noodles are tender, drain the water. Set noodles aside to cool to room temperature. If they are not tender, pour some additional boiling water over them. Let sit for another 5 minutes or until tender.

Set up a wrapping station to begin rolling. A wooden cutting board or a polyester dinner napkin works best with the rice-paper wrappers.

Lay out all of your prepared vegetables and cellophane noodles within close reach. Pour tepid water into a shallow dish large enough to soak the wrappers for your completed rolls. Have a plate nearby to put your completed spring rolls on. If you live in an arid climate, cover the finished rolls with plastic wrap while you work to keep the rolls from drying out.

To assemble, gently submerge one wrapper in the water for 5 to 10 seconds. It should feel firm and slightly sticky and will continue to soften as you add your filling. Lay the wrapper on your rolling surface and begin filling it with healthy pinches of each component, starting in the middle of the half closest to you. Put the flower petals down first and cover them with the basil and cilantro. This gives a great contrast when rolled up. Adding two avocado slices works best.

When you have added all your filling, bring the edge of the wrapper closest to you up and on top of the filling. When rolling the bundle, keep it tight. When the wrapper comes around to meet itself, fold over the two ends, again keeping it tight, and finish rolling.

If by this time the end of the wrapper is not very soft or sticky, wet your fingers and rub the end until it softens. This usually means your water is not warm enough or you are not soaking it enough before you begin. Cut in half on the bias and serve immediately with dipping sauce. Yields 12 to 15 rolls.

CHALLAH
Carri Ellis, Halleluyah Honey

---

8 cups flour, plus extra for working	¼ cup vegetable oil
1 ½ teaspoons salt	½ cup honey
1 tablespoon yeast	2 ½ cups warm water
3 eggs, divided	sesame or poppy seeds

Sift together flour, salt, and yeast into a very large mixing bowl. In a separate bowl, beat 2 eggs, then add vegetable oil, honey, and warm water, whisking each to combine before adding the next.

Add wet ingredients a bit at a time to dry ingredients, first stirring, then kneading as dough begins to form. Knead until dough is elastic and pliable and not sticky. Cover with a kitchen towel and put in a warm place to rise for 1 hour.

After dough rises, punch it down, and turn onto a clean, floured work surface, dividing the dough into 2 portions. Knead each portion a few minutes, adding a bit of flour, as necessary, to keep from sticking.

Divide each portion into 3 lengths. Pinch the lengths together at one end, and braid them, working from the middle.

Flour the bottoms of both braided loaves and place apart on a large, greased cooking sheet or on 2 separate sheets. Beat the remaining 1 egg, then evenly brush it across the tops of each braided loaf. Sprinkle seeds on the brushed braids and return them to a warm place to rise for about 40 minutes.

Preheat oven to 350 degrees while bread is rising. Bake for 30 to 40 minutes, rotating at least once. Loaves are done when golden brown, and they sound hollow when their bottoms are thumped. Makes 2 large braided loaves.

KOHLRABI LATKES
Michael Janik, michaelsapples.com

Latkes

3 (2-inch diameter) kohlrabi

½ medium onion, finely diced

1 large egg, beaten

2 tablespoons flour

3 tablespoons cooking oil or schmaltz

salt and pepper, to taste

sour cream (optional)

Note: Kohlrabi tastes similar to a broccoli stem or cabbage heart but milder and sweeter. It's quite unusual looking, and people often say it looks like an alien. It can be eaten raw or cooked. Give it a try!

Cut off root and leaves of kohlrabi. Peel and grate the bulb. Put kohlrabi and onion into a bowl; add egg and mix. Add flour and mix all ingredients. If too runny, add more flour.

Heat oil in a skillet until a drop of water sizzles and pops. Scoop a heaping tablespoon of mixture into the skillet. Flatten to make a pancake about 3 inches in diameter.

Cook several at the same time but do not crowd them in the pan. Cook until golden brown on the bottom; flip and cook the other side until golden brown. Drain on a paper towel. Serve as is or topped with sour cream. Can be used as an entrée or as a side dish.

CREAMY TURNIP SOUP
Randy Treichler, Star Hollow Farm

1 tablespoon butter

1 cup coarsely chopped onion

4 cups turnips (approximately 2 pounds), peeled and chopped

3 cups vegetable stock

2 tablespoons fresh parsley, minced

1 tablespoon sugar

1 tablespoon lemon juice

1 bay leaf

⅛ teaspoon black pepper

1 cup milk

½ teaspoon salt

2 tablespoons cream (optional)

Note: If you think you don't like turnips, you may change your mind after trying this soup!

Melt butter in a soup pot over low heat. Add onions and cook 5 to 10 minutes until soft and translucent. Stir in turnips, 2 cups of stock, parsley, sugar, lemon juice, bay leaf, and pepper.

Cover and simmer until turnips are tender, about 15 to 20 minutes. Stir occasionally and add additional stock as needed. Remove bay leaf.

Blend ingredients by placing vegetables in a food processor or blend with a hand-held immersion blender. Return ingredients to pot.

Add the milk and salt and heat just to boiling. If desired, add cream. Serve immediately. Makes 4 bowls.

PORTUGUESE KALE AND SAUSAGE SOUP
Sarah James

¼ cup olive oil

2 medium onions, finely chopped

4 cloves garlic, minced

3 medium potatoes, peeled and
  thinly sliced

6 cups chicken or vegetable broth

¾ pound kielbasa or other cooked
  sausage, cut into ½-inch slices

1 bunch kale, thick stems removed,
  thinly chopped

salt and pepper, to taste

olive oil (optional)

Parmesan cheese (optional)

Heat olive oil in a large soup pot over medium heat. Add the onions and sauté until lightly browned, 5 to 7 minutes. Add the garlic and cook for 1 minute longer. Add the potatoes, toss to coat, and sauté for 2 minutes longer. Add the stock, cover, and bring to a boil.

Reduce the heat to simmer and cook until the potatoes are tender, about 20 minutes. Remove from heat and cool slightly. You can mash some of the vegetables in the soup by hand or purée the soup in a blender. Leave it a little chunky if you like it that way.

Add the sausage, return to medium heat, and simmer until the sausage is heated through, about 5 minutes. Add the kale and cook, uncovered, until wilted and tender, 3 to 5 minutes. Season to taste with salt and pepper. Ladle the soup into warmed bowl and drizzle with olive oil. Sprinkle with Parmesan cheese if you choose. Serves 6.

SORREL SOUP
Randy Treichler, Star Hollow Farm

1 ½ tablespoons butter	3 to 4 cups stock or water
1 small onion, finely chopped	¼ cup sour cream (optional)
½ pound potatoes, peeled and cubed	salt and pepper, to taste
1 ½ cups tightly packed sorrel, stems removed (3 ounces)	lemon juice, to taste (optional)

Note: Fresh sorrel has a tart, tangy flavor. You can store leftover soup in the refrigerator. It makes a refreshing drink—like a green V8.

In a heavy pot, melt butter and sauté onion until soft but not brown. Add potatoes, sorrel, and 3 cups of stock or water.

Bring to boil. Reduce heat, cover, and simmer 10 to 15 minutes, until vegetables are very soft. Cool soup and purée until smooth in food processor or with immersion blender. Thin with more stock if needed. Add sour cream, lemon juice, salt, and pepper to taste.

Heat through; do not boil. Serve warm, or you can chill and serve cold. Serves 4.

• • •

CREAMY SPRING SOUP
Betty Phelan

4 cups chicken broth	2 garlic cloves, pressed
8 asparagus spears, trimmed and cut into 2-inch pieces	dash of pepper
	1 ½ cups cooked elbow macaroni
4 carrots, julienned	1 cup half & half (or milk)
1 celery rib, chopped fine	1 ½ cups fresh baby spinach, chopped
2 green onions, chopped	

In a large saucepan, combine broth, asparagus, carrots, celery, green onions, garlic, and pepper. Bring to a boil. Reduce heat. Cover and simmer for 5 to 10 minutes or until vegetables are tender. Stir in cooked macaroni, half & half, and spinach. Heat through. Serves 4.

NAPA SALAD
Nadine Malcolm

---

4 cups Napa cabbage, washed
   and chopped

4 cups lettuce (romaine, butter, red,
   or green leaf), washed and torn, or
   chopped into bite-size pieces

2 tablespoons sesame oil

2 tablespoons honey

4 teaspoons soy sauce

juice and zest of one lemon

¼ cup walnuts, almonds, dried cherries,
   dried cranberries or a combination

Note: Farm and ranch families comprise just two percent of the U.S. population. It's important to support our local farmers.

Place chopped cabbage and lettuce in a large bowl and mix together. In a small bowl, whisk together the oil, honey, soy sauce, lemon juice, and zest. Pour dressing over the greens mixture and toss. Divide into 4 salad bowls and top each with the dried fruit and nuts. Serves 4.

• • •

BROCCOLI SALAD
Cathy Sapata

---

1 cup mayonnaise

½ cup sugar

2 tablespoons vinegar

2 bunches raw broccoli, chopped into
   small pieces

½ cup pecans, coarsely chopped

1 cup cran-raisins

1 small red onion, chopped

Note: This is my cousin's variation on an old recipe from our family cookbook. The original recipe called for raisins and sunflower seeds, but I prefer this one.

Combine mayonnaise, sugar, and vinegar until well mixed. Mix in remaining ingredients. Chill at least 3 hours before serving. Serves 6.

KALE AND MIXED GREENS SALAD
Lara Ritchie, Nothing to It Culinary Center

For vinaigrette

2 tablespoons balsamic vinegar

1 tablespoon unseasoned rice wine vinegar

1 tablespoon honey

1 teaspoon Dijon mustard

2 tablespoons extra-virgin olive oil

salt and pepper, to taste

For salad and to serve

2 cups kale, rinsed, dried, and torn into small pieces

1 cup mixed greens, rinsed and dried

2 ½ tablespoons chiffonade of fresh basil (stack basil leaves, roll up into "cigars," and slice crosswise into ribbons)

1 cup sunflower shoots, cut into small pieces

1 small wedge aged Gouda cheese, shaved

¼ cup sunflower seeds, toasted

In a small bowl, whisk together the first 5 vinaigrette ingredients. Season with salt and pepper, to taste, and whisk again. Taste and then adjust seasoning if necessary.

In a large bowl, mix the kale, mixed greens, basil, sunflower shoots, Gouda, and sunflower seeds. Add some vinaigrette to the greens and toss. Taste to desired flavor and coating, adding more dressing if desired. Toss again. Serves 4.

MAPLE-BACON DRIZZLED SPINACH APPLE SALAD
Peri & Sons Farms

1 tablespoon pure maple syrup

1 teaspoon red wine vinegar

¼ teaspoon Dijon mustard

1 tablespoon olive oil

1 tablespoon fresh chives, chopped

¼ teaspoon salt

¼ teaspoon black pepper

2 slices bacon, cooked and crumbled

2 ½ cups julienne-cut Granny Smith apples (about 2 apples)

¼ cup red onion, sliced thin vertically

1 ounce crumbled Feta cheese

6 ounces baby spinach, washed

Whisk together maple syrup, red wine vinegar, and mustard in a small bowl. Gradually add oil, stirring with whisk until well blended.

Add chives, salt, pepper, and bacon; stir with a whisk until well blended. Combine apple, onion, cheese, and spinach in a large bowl. Drizzle with vinaigrette and toss to coat. Serve immediately. Serves 4.

CARAMELIZED ONION BREAKFAST BAKE
Peri & Sons Farms

6 strips thick-sliced bacon

3 cups fresh spinach, roughly chopped

1 large sweet onion, thinly sliced

5 eggs

1 cup milk

½ teaspoon fresh thyme

¼ teaspoon salt

¼ teaspoon pepper

4 ounces Swiss cheese, shredded

3 cups ciabatta or other dense bread cut into ½-inch cubes

Note: This dish can be prepared ahead of time and stored covered in the refrigerator overnight.

Preheat oven to 350 degrees. In a large skillet, cook the bacon until crisp. (Reserve the bacon drippings.)

Put the bacon on a paper towel. Once cooled, chop and spread bacon across the bottom of a 2-quart baking dish.

Using a small amount of the bacon drippings, in the same skillet, quickly sauté the spinach just until it is wilted. Spoon spinach over bacon in the baking dish.

Using the remaining bacon drippings, add the rings of sweet onion to the skillet and slowly cook over medium heat, removing them as soon as they turn a rich caramel brown color. Set aside.

In a medium bowl, hand whip the eggs, milk, thyme, salt, and pepper until well combined. Stir in the cheese. Pour the mixture on top of the bacon and spinach.

Distribute the bread cubes across the dish, pushing them into the mixture. Spread the caramelized onions across the top of the dish.

Bake for about 40 minutes, until set and lightly browned on top. Let stand 10 minutes before serving. Serves 6.

CHARD PIE
Erica Petersen

---

1 ½ cups chopped onion

1 tablespoon green or regular garlic, minced

2 tablespoons olive oil

1 bunch chard, chopped

8 eggs

2 cups milk or half & half

1 teaspoon salt

2 (8-inch) deep-dish pie shells

2 cups cheddar or Swiss cheese, grated

Add a 2-cup mixture of chopped ham, cooked bacon, diced tomatoes, chopped basil, or any veggies or meat (optional)

1 to 2 tablespoons fresh or dried dill weed (optional)

Preheat oven to 400 degrees. Sauté onions and garlic in olive oil over medium heat until soft. Add chard and cook until wilted.

Turn off heat and allow mixture to cool. Beat eggs, milk, and salt in a bowl. Spread chard mixture in the bottom of the pie shells. Add cheese to the top of the chard. Pour egg mixture over the top. Add one or more of the optional ingredients if desired. Sprinkle with dill weed (optional).

Bake for 30 to 40 minutes or until toothpick inserted into the center of the pies comes out clean. Makes 2 pies.

DR. DEETKEN'S SPINACH CASSEROLE
Michelle Deetken

4 to 5 cups spinach or mixed cooking
   greens, lightly chopped

1 cup celery, sliced

1 cup mushrooms, cleaned and sliced

½ cup green onions, chopped

1 teaspoon garlic powder

salt to taste

1 teaspoon black pepper

1 ½ cups grated cheddar cheese, divided

1 ½ cups grated Monterey Jack cheese,
   divided

½ cup sour cream

2 to 3 eggs, lightly beaten

½ cup Parmesan cheese, grated

1 cup cooked brown rice

Note: Nevada ranks eighth in the nation for onion production.

Preheat oven to 350 degrees. In a large bowl, mix spinach, celery, mushrooms, green onions, garlic powder, salt, and pepper. Lightly mix in 1 cup cheddar and 1 cup Monterey Jack cheese. Add sour cream and stir to coat evenly. Add beaten eggs and mix thoroughly to incorporate.

Press ½ cup of the cooked brown rice in an even layer on bottom of a 2-quart casserole dish. Add half of the spinach mixture and press out evenly. Add the remaining ½ cup of cooked brown rice and press out evenly.

Add the remainder of the spinach mixture and press out evenly. Finally, sprinkle the remaining cheddar, Monterey Jack, and Parmesan cheese evenly across the top spinach layer.

Bake 40 to 45 minutes, until the top of the casserole is light golden in color. Let sit 5 to 10 minutes before serving. If desired, casserole can be doubled and baked in a 4-quart casserole dish. Serves 4 to 6.

SPINACH, SWEET ONION, AND NOODLE CASSEROLE
Bunny Snyder, Snyder Family Farms

1 (12-ounce) package of medium egg noodles

2 tablespoons butter, melted

1 cup Swiss cheese, grated

salt and pepper, to taste

6 tablespoons butter, divided

2 sweet onions, diced

2 pounds fresh spinach, chopped, cooked, and drained (about 2 cups cooked)

1 cup breadcrumbs

1 hard-boiled egg, chopped

Preheat oven to 350 degrees. Cook noodles according to package directions, al dente, and drain. In a large bowl, toss cooked noodles, 2 tablespoons melted butter, Swiss cheese, salt, and pepper.

Steam the 2 pounds of fresh spinach until it is cooked down (about 2 cups). Drain, if necessary.

Melt 3 tablespoons of butter in a medium skillet. Add onions and cook over medium heat until soft. Stir in the cooked spinach. Raise the heat to medium high and cook for a couple minutes, until most of the moisture has evaporated, stirring often.

Butter a 2-quart baking dish. First, arrange ⅓ of the noodles on the bottom and cover with half of the spinach mixture. Next, place a second layer of noodles and apply the last of the spinach mixture. Finally, top your casserole with the remaining noodles.

Melt the remaining 3 tablespoons of butter in the skillet and stir in the breadcrumbs. Sprinkle over the casserole and bake for 30 minutes or until browned. Sprinkle with the chopped egg just before serving. Serves 6.

BAKED BEET AND CARROT BURGERS
Tina Smith

½ cup sesame seeds

1 cup sunflower seeds

2 cups beets, peeled and grated

2 cups carrots, peeled and grated

½ cup onion, minced

2 eggs, lightly beaten

1 cup cooked brown rice

1 cup cheddar cheese, grated

½ cup olive oil

3 tablespoons flour

½ cup Italian (flat-leaf) parsley, finely chopped

2 tablespoons soy sauce or tamari

1 clove garlic, minced

⅛ to ¼ teaspoon cayenne pepper, to taste

salt and black pepper, to taste

Preheat oven to 350 degrees. Brown sesame seeds in a skillet over low to medium heat for 3 to 5 minutes. Transfer to a dish. Repeat the process for the sunflower seeds. Combine beets, carrots, and onion in a large bowl.

Stir in the toasted seeds, eggs, rice, cheese, oil, flour, parsley, soy sauce, and garlic. Add cayenne and salt and black pepper, to taste. Mix with your hands—they work best. Shape mixture into 8 patties, and place on an oiled baking sheet.

Bake until brown around the edges, 20 to 30 minutes. Flip after 10 minutes to brown both sides. Serve alone or on your favorite toasted hamburger or sandwich bun, along with your favorite condiments. Serves 8.

PASTA WITH SAUSAGE AND SWISS CHARD
Sarah Smith

---

2 cloves garlic, minced

6 tablespoons olive oil

6 ounces of your favorite sausage

1 pound of your favorite pasta

1 bunch swiss chard, stalks removed and leaves thinly sliced

Parmesan or Romano cheese, grated, to taste

4 tablespoons olive oil

Sauté garlic in olive oil over medium heat until golden, about 5 minutes. Be careful not to burn it. Add your favorite sausage. Crumble the meat and cook it until done, but do not let it brown. Set aside.

Meanwhile, cook your favorite pasta. Just when the pasta is cooked almost al dente, add the chard. Cook until tender, only a few minutes. Drain pasta and chard together, then add to the frying pan with the sausage. Finish cooking for about two minutes.

Serve with freshly grated Parmesan or Romano cheese and olive oil, all tossed together. Serves 6.

LAMB SHANKS IN WINE SAUCE
Nancy Guntly-Smith, Smith Ranch

6 lamb shanks	**Sauce**
salt and pepper, to taste	1 cup water
garlic salt	3 tablespoons Worcestershire sauce
your favorite herbs and seasonings	½ cup red wine
	½ cup red wine vinegar
	4 garlic cloves, diced

Note: This is an old family recipe.

Preheat oven to 350 degrees. Sear the lamb shanks on the stovetop or barbecue on both sides. Season with salt, pepper, garlic salt, and your favorite seasonings. Place shanks in a roasting pan. Mix the water, Worcestershire sauce, wine, vinegar, and garlic. Pour over the lamb in the roaster.

Cover and bake for 2 to 3 hours. Turn the shanks several times during cooking to keep them well coated. The sauce is wonderful served over polenta or potatoes. Serves 6.

GREEK-STYLE LEG OF LAMB
Constantine and Susan Georgioua

---

1 leg of lamb, bone in (5 to 9 pounds)	1 tablespoon freshly ground black pepper
1 head of garlic, peeled	2 cups water
½ cup fresh lemon juice (3 to 4 lemons)	6 medium potatoes, peeled and cut in half
3 tablespoons dried oregano	

Note: A Greek cucumber salad is the perfect side dish for this recipe.

Preheat oven to 325 degrees. Cut small slits in the leg of lamb and insert garlic into slits. Space garlic evenly throughout the lamb.

Place lamb in large roasting pan and pour lemon juice generously into the garlic slits and over the lamb. Generously sprinkle the top half of the lamb with half of the oregano and half the black pepper. Pour a cup of water into the bottom of the pan. Bake uncovered, basting every 30 minutes.

Turn after one hour, and add remaining oregano and pepper to the top of the lamb. Add potatoes during the last hour, placing them around the lamb. Add a second cup of water to the bottom of the pan.

Bake for 20 to 30 minutes per pound of meat to desired doneness. Test with a meat thermometer: 145 degrees for medium, 160 degrees for well-done. Do not cook over 160 degrees. Serves 6.

CHOCOLATE BEET BUNDT CAKE
Christine Mehring, Blue Lizard Farm

cooking spray

½ cup granulated sugar

½ cup butter, room temperature, divided

1 cup light brown sugar, packed

2 tablespoons honey

4 large eggs

1 ½ cups puréed cooked beets

1 teaspoon vanilla

1 cup semi-sweet chocolate chips

1 ¼ cup flour

½ cup cocoa powder

1 ½ teaspoons baking soda

1 teaspoon salt

Preheat oven to 375 degrees. Prepare Bundt pan by spraying evenly with cooking spray. Dust the inside of the pan completely with granulated sugar, dumping out any excess that does not stick to the spray. Set aside.

Remove 2 tablespoons of the butter and set aside. In a large mixing bowl, combine the remaining butter, brown sugar, and honey. Beat until light and creamy. Add eggs one at a time, beating after each addition. Add beets and vanilla, stirring to combine.

In a microwave-safe bowl, combine the chocolate chips and 2 tablespoons of butter. Melt together just until the chips soften. Stir until smooth and add to the mixing bowl. Beat well to combine.

In a separate bowl, sift together the flour, cocoa powder, baking soda, and salt. Stir into the beet mixture until well combined and smooth. Batter will be thick.

Pour into the prepared Bundt pan. Bake for 30 to 35 minutes until a toothpick inserted into center comes out clean. Cool in pan for 15 minutes, then turn out carefully on to a serving plate. This is a dense, moist cake. The resting time is important so that the cake does not stick to the pan. No frosting is needed. Serves 12.

HONEY CAKE
Debbie Gilmore, Hall's Honey

3 eggs, separated	½ teaspoon baking soda
½ cup butter	½ teaspoon salt
¾ cup honey	½ teaspoon cinnamon
½ cup sugar	½ cup cocoa
1 teaspoon vanilla	¾ cup cold-brewed coffee
1 ⅓ cups flour	½ cup walnuts, chopped

Note: This is an old family recipe from my grandmother. My family has been beekeeping for five generations, since 1918.

Preheat oven to 350 degrees. Separate eggs, placing yolks in a large bowl and the whites in a smaller bowl. Beat the egg whites with an electric mixer until they form stiff peaks.

To the large bowl, add butter, honey, sugar ,and vanilla to egg yolks. Cream thoroughly. Sift the dry ingredients together, and add to the creamed mixture, alternating with the coffee. Stir in nuts. Fold in beaten egg whites.

Pour into a lightly oiled 9"x13" pan. Bake for 25 to 35 minutes or until a toothpick inserted into the center comes out clean. Serves 20.

RHUBARB CAKE
Brenda Smith, Smith & Smith Farms

Cake

1 ½ cups rhubarb, cut into ½-inch slices

½ cup sugar

2 cups flour

1 ½ cups sugar

1 teaspoon baking soda

½ teaspoon salt

1 teaspoon cinnamon

½ cup oil

1 egg

1 cup buttermilk

1 teaspoon vanilla

Frosting

6 tablespoons butter

1 cup coconut

⅔ cup brown sugar

¼ cup milk

1 cup chopped walnuts or pecans

Note: For the best flavor, make this cake 24 hours before serving.

Cake

Preheat oven to 350 degrees. Mix rhubarb and ½ cup sugar; set aside. In a separate bowl, combine flour, remaining 1 ½ cups sugar, baking soda, salt, and cinnamon.

Mix the oil, egg, buttermilk, and vanilla. Mix in the dry ingredients and rhubarb. Pour into greased and floured 9"x13" baking pan. Bake approximately 60 minutes or until a toothpick inserted into center of cake comes out clean. Frost while warm.

Frosting

Combine butter, coconut, brown sugar, and milk in saucepan. Cook over low heat for approximately 3 minutes. Stir in nuts. Spread over warm cake. Serves 20.

RHUBARB TORTE
Susan Emmons

Crust

2 cups all-purpose flour

2 tablespoons sugar

1 cup butter, cold

Filling

6 egg yolks (save egg whites for meringue)

2 cups sugar

¼ cup all-purpose flour

⅛ teaspoon salt

5 cups rhubarb, finely chopped

1 cup whole milk or half & half

Meringue

6 egg whites, room temperature

⅛ teaspoon cream of tartar

¾ cup sugar

Crust
Preheat oven to 350 degrees. Oil a 9"x13" baking pan. Combine flour and sugar; cut in butter until crumbly. Press into the prepared pan. Bake for 10 to 15 minutes or until lightly browned. Cool on a wire rack.

Filling
In a large bowl, beat egg yolks. Add sugar, flour, and salt. Stir in rhubarb and milk. Pour over the crust. Bake for 50 to 60 minutes or until a knife inserted near the center comes out clean. Prepare meringue for top of torte.

Meringue
In a large bowl, use an electric mixer to beat the egg whites and cream of tartar on medium speed, until soft peaks form. Gradually beat in the sugar, 1 tablespoon at a time, until stiff peaks form. Immediately spread over hot filling, sealing edges. Bake for 15 minutes or until slightly browned. Cool for at least 1 hour before serving. Refrigerate leftovers. Serves 16.

SUMMER

QUICK PICO DE GALLO
Katie Little

2 cups tomatoes, diced

½ medium onion, diced

2 cloves garlic, minced, or more,
   to taste

1 jalapeño pepper, diced

a few sprigs of cilantro, chopped

juice of 2 limes

salt, to taste

Note: Onions should be stored in a cool, dark, well-ventilated place away from other produce. Moisture in the refrigerator will turn onions soft, and onions have a tendency to impart their flavor to surrounding foods.

Mix together all ingredients in a medium mixing bowl. Chill for at least one hour to allow flavors to blend. Serve with tortilla chips. Serves 4.

• • •

HONEY MUSTARD DRESSING
Karen Foster, Hidden Valley Honey

½ cup local honey

½ cup Dijon mustard

½ cup mayonnaise

½ teaspoon Worcestershire sauce

Note: This is good on green salads, including spinach salads.

Heat the honey slightly, then whisk in a bowl with the rest of the ingredients.
Store in refrigerator.

RASPBERRY POPPYSEED VINAIGRETTE DRESSING
B. Ann Lattin, Lattin Farms

Raspberry Vinegar

3 cups cider vinegar

1 cup fresh raspberries

2 tablespoons white sugar

Poppyseed Dressing

1 ½ cups raspberry vinegar

1 cup olive oil

1 cup sugar (may use less or use Splenda)

1 tablespoon salt

1 ½ teaspoons dry mustard

1 purple onion, chopped

2 tablespoons poppy seeds

Note: This vinaigrette is wonderful on mixed salad greens. It is a favorite at Lattin Farms when raspberries are in season.

Raspberry Vinegar

Combine vinegar, berries, and sugar in a medium glass bowl. Mix gently and pour mixture into a large glass jar. Cover tightly and store at room temperature. It is best to let mixture sit for a week or longer to ripen. Strain berries from vinegar before using.

Poppyseed Dressing

Combine the vinegar, oil, sugar, salt, dry mustard, and onion in a blender. Mix well. Remove from blender, add the poppy seeds, and mix well. Keep refrigerated.

PEAR SALAD WITH LEMON DRESSING
Nadine Malcolm

Salad

6 cups lettuce, torn or chopped into
  bite-sized pieces

1 ½ cups cabbage, chopped

¾ cup diced cooked beets or chopped red
  bell peppers

1 large pear or 2 small pears, diced (the
  red ones add color)

2 tablespoons finely shredded sharp
  cheddar cheese

Dressing

2 tablespoons extra-virgin olive oil

2 tablespoons fresh lemon juice

1 tablespoon honey

½ teaspoon grated ginger root

Note: The color of local honey is determined by where the hives are located and what plants the bees were eating. Colors can range from light to dark, and they're all good.

In a large bowl, toss the lettuce, cabbage, and your choice of beets or bell peppers. Save the pears and cheese for later.

In a small bowl, whisk together the olive oil, lemon juice, honey, and ginger root. Add the dressing to the lettuce mixture in the large bowl and toss to coat. Gently toss in the diced pears. Divide the salad into 4 bowls and top each with grated cheese. Serves 4.

ROASTED EGGPLANT AND FETA DIP
Hazel Gomes

---

1 medium eggplant (about 1 pound)

1 tablespoon fresh lemon juice

¼ cup extra-virgin olive oil

½ cup feta cheese, crumbled

½ cup red onion, finely chopped

1 small red bell pepper, finely chopped

1 small chile pepper (such as jalapeño), seeded and minced

2 tablespoons fresh basil, chopped

1 tablespoon flat-leaf parsley, finely chopped

¼ teaspoon cayenne pepper (more or less to taste)

¼ teaspoon salt

pinch of sugar (optional)

Position oven rack about 6 inches from the heat source, and preheat broiler. Line a baking pan with foil.

Place eggplant in the pan, and poke a few holes all over it to vent steam. Broil the eggplant, turning with tongs every 5 minutes until the skin is charred and a knife inserted into the flesh near the stem goes in easily, 14 to 18 minutes.

Transfer to a cutting board. When it is cool enough to handle, cut the eggplant in half lengthwise and scrape the flesh into a medium-sized bowl. Add lemon juice and mix eggplant with the juice to help prevent discoloring. Add oil and stir with a fork until the oil is absorbed — there is no need to use a mixer or blender.

Stir in feta cheese, onion, bell pepper, chile pepper, basil, parsley, cayenne pepper, and salt. Taste and add sugar if desired. Serve with crackers or fresh vegetables. Makes about 2 cups.

GRILLED CANTALOUPE WITH
GINGER BLUEBERRY SAUCE
Nancy Horn, Dish Café

Sauce

2 cups fresh blueberries

¼ cup local honey

1-inch knob fresh ginger, peeled and
  minced very fine

1 teaspoon fresh lemon juice

1 teaspoon vanilla extract

2 tablespoons water

For cantaloupe and to serve

2 small cantaloupes

2 tablespoons granulated sugar

fresh mint leaves for garnish

vanilla ice cream or frozen yogurt
  (optional)

Note: Cool leftover sauce to room temperature and store in the refrigerator for up to one week. The sauce also can be frozen in an airtight, resealable freezer bag with the air pressed out. Some of the gorgeous sauce spooned into a pretty jar with a little note and a ribbon makes a fun and festive gift.

Sauce

In a small saucepan over medium heat, combine blueberries, honey, ginger, lemon juice, vanilla extract, and water. Bring to a boil and boil for 8 to 10 minutes, stirring every few minutes until thickened.

Remove from heat. Sauce should be thick, kind of like fruity jam, with some of the berries burst and some whole. Taste and add more honey if you like. Makes 2 cups.

For cantaloupe and to serve

Wash cantaloupes. Cut in half and core to remove seeds. Slice into wedges, leaving the rind on.

Heat a grill pan to high (if cooking indoors) or heat the outdoor grill to high. Sprinkle the fruit with sugar.

When the pan or grill is very, very hot, lay the melon down and grill each side of melon flesh (not the rind) about 1 minute, just until you see some grill marks. Divide wedges among plates and serve with sauce alongside.

Garnish with fresh mint. If you like, add a scoop of vanilla ice cream or frozen yogurt. Serves 4 to 6.

MELON SKEWERS WITH CHILE POWDER
Laura Longero Holman

1 cantaloupe, any size

Mexican red chile powder

Note: Red chile powder is different from the chili powder you find in stores. Red chile powder is pure ground chile pods without any additives, while chili powder often has other spices added.

Wash cantaloupe and cut in half. Remove the seeds and rind and cut into wedges. Cut flesh into 1-inch cubes and skewer with wooden skewers. Sprinkle with Mexican red chile powder. Serve fresh. Serves 4.

• • •

CANTALOUPE SMOOTHIE
Nancy Horn, Dish Café

½ ripe cantaloupe, peeled, seeded, and cut into chunks

1 cup milk

1 cup plain yogurt

1 cup crushed ice

2 tablespoons honey or sugar

Note: Hearts of Gold cantaloupe are the cantaloupe that made Fallon famous. They are heirloom cantaloupes and enjoyed peak sales in the 1950s, when they were shipped across the United States to fine-dining establishments in New York City. Today, you'll find them at farmers markets and at the Fallon Cantaloupe Festival every September.

Combine ingredients in a blender until smooth. Makes about 4 cups.

SORREL PINEAPPLE SMOOTHIES
Christine Mehring, Blue Lizard Farm

1 cup of cold water	1 cup fresh or frozen pineapple chunks
1 handful-sized bunch of fresh sorrel leaves and stems, washed	5 to 6 ice cubes
	sweetener of choice, to taste
½ ripe avocado	

Note: I love sorrel in smoothies. Sorrel is a leafy green with a distinctly tart, lemony flavor. Unlike many greens (ahem... kale...) with flavors and textures that require additional ingredients to make a tasty drink, sorrel shines with little encouragement and is wonderfully refreshing on a hot afternoon. Sorrel is high in vitamins A and C and is a good source of many B vitamins, potassium, and manganese. Please note that people who are prone to kidney stones need to be careful with sorrel, as it contains oxalic acid. Because sorrel is so good on its own, I like to keep these smoothies simple.

Pour water in blender and feed the leaves in a couple at a time. When they are liquefied, add the rest of the ingredients. Blend until smooth and creamy. Makes about one quart, so you have plenty to share...or not.

• • •

WARM BALSAMIC COUSCOUS SALAD
Justin Bart, Renown Health

1 tablespoon olive oil	½ cup shredded carrots
1 clove garlic, minced	3 cups cooked couscous
1 pound yellow squash or zucchini or a combination, coarsely grated	1 tablespoon balsamic vinegar
	salt and pepper, to taste
1 cup sliced mushrooms	¼ cup chopped fresh basil

Heat the olive oil in a skillet over medium heat. Add garlic and cook for 30 seconds, stirring constantly. Add the squash, carrots, and mushrooms. Cook, stirring frequently, until squash and mushrooms are tender. Stir in the couscous and vinegar. Heat through. Season to taste. Stir in the basil just before serving. Serves 4.

SUMMER BREAD SALAD
WITH ZUCCHINI, TOMATOES, AND FETA
Arianne Johnson

1 ½ cups thinly sliced zucchini

1 ½ cups chopped tomatoes

½ cup crumbled feta cheese

¼ cup chopped sweet or green onion

⅓ cup chopped olives of choice

¼ to ½ cup chopped fresh basil

¼ cup olive oil

3 tablespoons white or red wine vinegar or vinegar of choice

2 tablespoons minced garlic

salt and black pepper, freshly ground, to taste

5 to 6 cups firm-textured bread cubes, dried or toasted

Note: Tomatoes can be kept frozen for up to 12 months after being picked.

In a large bowl, combine all ingredients except bread. Let mixture stand at room temperature to develop flavor for 30 minutes to 1 hour, tossing occasionally. Mix in bread cubes just before serving. Serves 6.

FRIED ZUCCHINI SALAD
WITH TOMATOES AND GARLIC
Arnold Carbone, Glorious Garlic Farm

3 tablespoons extra-virgin olive oil, divided

2 large garlic cloves, peeled and thinly sliced

1 medium (8- to 10-inch) zucchini, sliced into ¼-inch thick slices

½ cup cherry tomatoes, halved

2 tablespoons diced green bell pepper

1 teaspoon fresh basil, finely chopped

red wine vinegar

sea salt

freshly ground black pepper

¼ cup Romano cheese, shaved

Note: This summer salad is a light, flavorful dish that goes well with a small side of pasta with pesto, garlic toast, and a nice, light, chilled red table wine.

Over medium heat, add 2 tablespoons olive oil to a medium-size, nonstick skillet.

Add garlic slices and cook on medium-low heat for no more than 5 minutes. This a bit tricky. It's important not to burn or brown the garlic. You're basically attempting to flavor the oil while keeping the garlic from dissolving. The garlic should be a light golden color and slightly translucent.

When the garlic is done, strain it from the oil and return the oil to skillet. Bring the heat up to medium-high on the newly flavored garlic oil, and layer the zucchini slices side by side in the pan. Brown on 1 side, about 1 minute. Flip and brown the other side.

Don't crowd the zucchini, or you will be steaming them. Repeat with remaining zucchini slices. Remove slices to paper towels to drain some of the oil from them. The hard part is done.

Place the cherry tomatoes, green pepper, basil, and reserved garlic in a large bowl. Drizzle with the remaining 1 tablespoon oil and a splash of red wine vinegar. Sprinkle with salt and black pepper and mix gently until well blended.

Place the zucchini on a serving dish and spoon the tomato and green-pepper blend over the top. Garnish with Romano cheese. Serves 2.

TRI-COLOR SALAD WITH QUESO FRESCO AND LIME-HONEY VINAIGRETTE

Isidro Alves, Sand Hill Dairy

Vinaigrette

2 tablespoons fresh lime juice

2 tablespoons white distilled vinegar

1 ½ teaspoons Dijon mustard

½ teaspoon honey or brown sugar

1 ½ teaspoons sea salt

½ teaspoon freshly ground black pepper

5 tablespoons vegetable oil

5 tablespoons olive oil

Salad

2 heads of Bibb or leaf lettuce, torn into bite-sized pieces

2 tomatoes, quartered

1 large avocado, pitted and sliced

8 ounces queso fresco, crumbled

Note: We make this salad with queso fresco, fresh from our artisan cheese dairy.

Vinaigrette
Combine lime juice, vinegar, Dijon mustard, honey, salt, and pepper in a bowl and whisk together. Slowly add vegetable oil and olive oil as you whisk. Set aside. Whisk again before using to recombine.

Salad
Combine lettuce leaves and tomatoes in a salad bowl. Add some of the vinaigrette and gently toss. Place the avocado slices and crumbled queso fresco on top. Drizzle a little more vinaigrette on top and serve. Serves 8 to 10.

TOMATO SALAD WITH WARM RICOTTA CHEESE
Tina Smith

2 pounds ricotta cheese

1 teaspoon salt

1 ¼ cups olive oil

1 teaspoon black pepper, coarsely ground

3 tablespoons diced shallots

3 tablespoons red wine vinegar

2 tablespoons sherry vinegar

salt and freshly ground black pepper, to taste

1 sprig basil

2 pounds tomatoes (mixed varieties and sizes, if desired)

3 tablespoons minced basil

Note: Fresh tomatoes are best stored at room temperature and away from sunlight. Refrigeration will stop the ripening process and damage membranes in the cell walls, resulting in soft, mealy tomatoes.

Preheat oven to 350 degrees. Mix cheese and 1 teaspoon salt together. Put mixture in a baking dish or casserole that is at least 8"x8".

Drizzle with ¼ cup of the olive oil and the 1 teaspoon coarsely ground pepper. Bake until browned on top and bubbly around the edges, about 20 minutes. Let sit about 10 minutes before serving.

Meanwhile, in a bowl, combine shallots, vinegars, basil sprig, and salt and pepper. Let sit 20 minutes. Discard basil sprig.

Whisk in the remaining 1 cup olive oil. Adjust flavor as desired, with additional vinegar, salt, and pepper.

Cut large tomatoes into halves or quarters; leave small ones whole. Add tomatoes to vinaigrette and toss to coat.

Divide the tomatoes among 6 salad plates. Add a spoonful of the warm ricotta to each. Scatter the minced basil over the top. Eat up with a crusty piece of bread! Serves 6.

SWEET AND SOUR SUMMER SQUASH SALAD
Virginia Gibbs

Salad	Dressing
4 small zucchini	1 cup white wine vinegar
4 small yellow squash	¾ cup sugar
3 stalks celery	⅓ cup vegetable oil
1 sweet red bell pepper	1 teaspoon salt
1 small red onion, finely chopped	1 teaspoon pepper

Note: Grate raw zucchini and freeze it in measured portions. Use a food processor or electric grater to save time on large quantities. In the winter, you can use the zucchini in breads, cakes, and casseroles. Squeeze out the excess moisture before using.

Slice zucchini, yellow squash, celery, and bell pepper paper-thin. Place in medium bowl with chopped onion. In a saucepan, combine vinegar, sugar, oil, salt, and pepper; bring to a boil.

Reduce heat and stir constantly until sugar is dissolved. Cool mixture, then pour over prepared vegetables. Cover and chill at least 4 hours. Serves 4.

BURRATA AND HEIRLOOM TOMATO SALAD
Chef Brett Uniss, Honey Salt Restaurant

3 heirloom tomatoes, cut into wedges

3 red grape tomatoes, halved

3 yellow grape tomatoes, halved

3 blood-orange segments

1 tablespoon olive oil

2 teaspoons balsamic vinegar

salt and pepper, to taste

3 ounces Burrata cheese

2 basil leaves, torn

1 teaspoon balsamic glaze or aged balsamic

Note: Burrata is a fresh Italian cheese made from mozzarella and cream. The outer shell is solid mozzarella, and the inside contains mozzarella and cream, giving it an unusual soft texture.

In a mixing bowl, season the tomatoes, red and yellow grape tomatoes, and blood-orange segments with the olive oil, balsamic vinegar, salt, and pepper. In the center of a plate, place the Burrata cheese and arrange the marinated tomatoes and oranges around it. Top with the torn basil leaves and garnish with the balsamic glaze. Serves 2.

• • •

NEVADA GOLD CUCUMBER SALAD
Bonda Young, Great Basin Brewing Company

2 tablespoons Nevada Gold (a Kolsch-style beer available at The Great Basin Brewing Company). If unavailable, substitute Continental or Bohemian Pilsner or a Märzen- or Vienna-style lager.

2 teaspoons olive oil

2 tablespoons white vinegar

2 to 3 teaspoons white sugar, to taste

¼ teaspoon salt

3 cups thinly sliced cucumbers

2 tablespoons chopped onion

1 tablespoon shredded carrots

Note: This is a light and tasty side dish that will complement many entrees that might lean a bit to the heavy side, such as fried foods, stews, or casseroles.

Combine beer, oil, and vinegar in a medium mixing bowl. Stir in sugar and salt until dissolved. Add cucumber, onion, and carrot. Marinate in the refrigerator for at least one hour. Serves 6.

JEN O'S SUMMER MEDLEY SALAD
Jennifer O'Sheroff

Salad	Dressing
4 to 5 medium assorted summer squash	¼ cup balsamic vinegar
1 to 2 teaspoons olive oil	⅔ cup extra-virgin olive oil
salt and pepper, to taste	1 tablespoon minced shallot
4 large heirloom or vine-ripe tomatoes	1 teaspoon fresh minced basil
8 ounces fresh mozzarella cheese	1 teaspoon minced thyme
½ red onion, sliced thin	1 teaspoon minced chives
5 to 6 cups fresh assorted salad greens	1 teaspoon minced parsley

Slice summer squash ¼-inch thick and toss with the olive oil, salt, and pepper. Heat an outdoor grill and grill lightly. If overcooked, they will become mushy. This can be done early in the day and set aside. Slice the squash again in semi-circles, and toss in a large bowl. Cut tomatoes into large chunks, and toss with the squash. Slice cheese in small chunks or thin slices, and add to the squash mixture. Place the salad greens in a separate large bowl and set aside.

Mix dressing ingredients in a small bowl. Toss a small amount of dressing on the greens; lay these out on a platter. Toss a bit more dressing with the vegetables and cheese. Pour these over the greens. Serves 6.

KACHUMBER
(Indian Tomato-Onion Salad)
Janet Carter

2 to 3 medium vine-ripened tomatoes, julienned

1 medium red onion, julienned

1 freshly picked green-garlic bulb and half of the stem, finely chopped

¾ teaspoon salt

½ teaspoon ground cumin

4 teaspoons sugar

¼ teaspoon ground black pepper

¼ cup chopped cilantro leaves

juice of one large lemon

Note: The green garlic bulb is optional if not in season, but it really is better with it!

In a large bowl, toss together tomatoes, onion, garlic, salt, cumin, sugar, pepper, cilantro, and lemon juice. Adjust seasonings to taste. Let salad stand for a few minutes so the juices mingle. Serves 4.

SUMMER TOMATO BRUSCHETTA
Laura Longero Holman

---

4 medium, ripe tomatoes, cored and diced

kosher salt and freshly ground black
pepper, to taste

8 thick slices of crusty firm Italian bread
or other country-style bread—focaccia
is my favorite

2 large cloves garlic, peeled and halved

3 to 4 tablespoons extra-virgin olive oil

½ cup fresh basil leaves, slivered

fresh Parmesan cheese, grated

Note: I prefer to use heirloom tomatoes for this recipe, and hopefully, your tomatoes have been stored at room temperature, as chilling kills their flavor. There are only a few ingredients, so all ingredients need to be at their peak.

(Recipe adapted by Laura Longero from *The Joy of Cooking* by Irma Rombauer).

Preheat the broiler. Combine the tomatoes, salt, and pepper in a small bowl. Let tomato mixture stand for 15 to 30 minutes so the tomatoes release their juices. Brush the bread slices with olive oil. Place the bread in the oven and broil, turning once, until golden brown, about 3 minutes each side. (If using focaccia, slice lengthwise and only toast the tops; otherwise the bread is too crunchy.)

Remove the bread from the heat, and rub the top with the halved garlic. Spoon the tomato mixture on top of the toast. Sprinkle with basil and freshly grated Parmesan to taste. Drizzle with olive oil. Sprinkle with extra salt if desired. Makes 8 slices.

STUFFED SQUASH BLOSSOMS

Diane Greene, Herbs by Diane

Batter	Cheese Stuffing
1 cup flour	¼ cup ricotta, goat, or cream cheese
½ cup cornstarch	1 garlic clove, minced
½ teaspoon salt	¼ teaspoon each salt and pepper
1 cup chilled milk, beer, or water	1 tablespoon basil or parsley, minced
	10 large squash blossoms
	canola oil for frying

Note: The best place to find squash blossoms is at your local farmers market.

Batter

Prepare the batter first. Sift together dry ingredients, then whisk in milk, beer, or cold water until smooth. Cover and set in the refrigerator for 30 minutes.

Cheese Stuffing

In a bowl, combine the cheese, garlic, salt, pepper, and basil. Open the blossoms and spoon about a ½ teaspoon of the mixture into the center of each. Avoid overfilling.

Twist the top of each blossom together to close. Place on a baking sheet and refrigerate for 15 minutes. Pour the oil in a skillet to a depth of ½ inch. Heat over high heat.

Dip each stuffed blossom into the batter and then into the hot oil. Cook until golden on all sides, about three minutes. Transfer with a slotted utensil to paper towels to drain briefly. Makes 10.

SMOKY CHILI CORN ON THE COB
Christine Bushgens

fresh ears of sweet corn, 1 per person

butter

pasilla chili powder

cumin

fresh lime juice

Note: This is not hot spicy, just delicious. Sometimes I use more chili powder than other times, depending on my mood. But be careful with the cumin. It can overpower the taste.

Shuck, rinse, and pat the corn dry. Spread butter on the cob. Sprinkle chili powder and cumin over the corn to taste. Some like it mild, some like it spicier. Wrap each cob in aluminum foil and cook over a barbecue at low temperature, turning them every 5 minutes for approximately 20 minutes, until tender. Before eating, squirt a little fresh lime juice over the corn.

• • •

NEVADA CORN STEW
Ann Louhela

1 pound ground beef

1 onion, coarsely chopped

1 clove garlic, finely chopped

1 green bell pepper, coarsely chopped

3 cups fresh corn, cut off the cob
(about 4 ears)

3 ripe tomatoes, peeled and coarsely chopped

1 tablespoon Worcestershire sauce

2 teaspoons sugar

1 ½ teaspoons salt

Note: This is a quick summer stew, and it's best made in a cast-iron kettle. You can change the vegetable ingredients based on what's in the garden or at the farmers market.

Sauté the ground beef in a large skillet over high heat until browned. Stir in the onion, garlic, and bell pepper and cook for about 5 to 7 minutes over medium heat, until onion is soft and translucent. Add the corn, tomatoes, Worcestershire sauce, sugar, and salt. Cover and simmer gently for about 30 minutes. Serves 4 to 6.

ZUCCHINI GARDEN CHOWDER
Don Delegal

1 ½ cups fresh corn, cut off the cob (about 2 to 3 ears)

2 medium zucchini, chopped into ½-inch pieces

1 medium onion, chopped

2 tablespoons fresh parsley, chopped

1 teaspoon fresh basil, chopped

⅓ cup butter

⅓ cup flour

1 teaspoon salt

dash of pepper

3 cups chicken or vegetable broth

1 teaspoon fresh lemon juice

1 (14-ounce) can diced tomatoes, undrained

1 ½ cups whole milk or half & half

pinch of sugar

¼ cup Parmesan cheese, grated

2 cups cheddar cheese, shredded

In a stock pot, sauté corn, zucchini, onion, parsley, and basil in butter until tender. Stir in flour, salt, and pepper to make a roux. Gradually stir in broth and lemon juice. Bring to a boil. Reduce heat and simmer for 2 minutes. Add tomatoes, milk, and sugar. Bring to a boil. Reduce heat; cover and simmer for 5 minutes or until vegetables are tender. Add cheeses just before serving.

SPICY CHICKEN SOUP
Sarah Smith

---

1 tablespoon butter

1 cup chopped onion

2 tablespoons chopped jalapeño pepper

1 ½ teaspoons ground cumin

1 teaspoon chili powder

2 cups fresh corn, cut from the cob

3 cups zucchini, sliced

2 cups finely chopped tomatoes

4 cups chicken broth

½ teaspoon salt

2 cups chopped boneless cooked chicken

2 tablespoons fresh lime juice

toasted corn tortilla strips

Melt butter in stock pot; add onion and jalapeño. Sauté until onion is tender. Add cumin, chili powder, corn, zucchini, tomatoes, broth, and salt. Bring mixture to a boil. Reduce heat and simmer for 20 to 30 minutes. Add cooked chicken and heat through. Remove from heat and add lime juice. Serve with toasted corn tortilla strips. Serves 4.

RATATOUILLE
Brandon Bryan, Old Granite Street Eatery

1 eggplant, large diced, stem and
skin removed

2 tablespoons salt

2 tablespoons olive oil

2 medium onions, large diced

5 cloves garlic, minced

2 medium zucchini, large diced

2 medium yellow squash, large diced

3 heirloom tomatoes, seeds removed,
large diced

2 tablespoons sherry vinegar

salt and pepper, to taste

Note: When composing a dish for an upcoming menu, I like to meet with local farmers to see what they have in abundance for the season. This recipe was inspired by Craig from City Green Gardens.

Place the eggplant in a mixing bowl. Toss with approximately 2 tablespoons salt and refrigerate for one hour. The salt will help remove excess moisture from the eggplant.

Place 2 tablespoons olive oil in a medium-sized pot and bring to medium-low heat. Place the onion and garlic in the pot and sauté until onion becomes translucent. Add the zucchini, yellow squash, and tomatoes.

Place eggplant in a kitchen towel and wring out the excess moisture; add to pot. Bring contents to a low simmer. Add sherry vinegar and salt and pepper to taste.

Cover and simmer for approximately one hour. If ratatouille is still soupy, remove the lid for last 10 minutes. Serves 4 to 6.

FRESH VEGGIE FRITTATA
Terry Bell, The Dutch Diva

---

2 cups fresh spinach leaves

2 cups fresh mushrooms, sliced

2 cups asparagus, cut into 1-inch pieces

2 cups peppers (red, yellow, green, or a combination), cut into strips

(You can use 8 cups of any combination of vegetables you like—these make a colorful dish)

12 eggs

2 cups milk

1 tablespoon garlic salt

2 teaspoons fresh basil

1 teaspoon fresh ground pepper

½ teaspoon red pepper flakes

1 cup grated cheddar cheese

1 cup grated pepper jack cheese

fresh cilantro, chopped

salsa

Note: This has been a favorite dish of mine for several years and is a great way to show off a variety of locally grown produce. Dutch-oven dishes are often heavy on packaged ingredients suitable for camping, but this dish shows the versatility of outdoor Dutch-oven cooking in a light and healthy way.

Generously grease a 12-inch Dutch oven. I like using Butter Flavor Crisco. Layer your vegetables in the oven. Beat together the eggs, milk, garlic salt, basil, pepper, and red pepper flakes. Pour mixture over the vegetables.

Bake at 350 degrees using 16 coals on the bottom and 18 on the top.* Bake for 40 minutes or until the egg mixture is set and firm.

Sprinkle cheddar and jack cheeses over the top and bake for an additional 10 to 15 minutes, until the cheese is melted and bubbly.

Garnish with freshly chopped cilantro and serve with salsa. Serves 8.

* *If using a conventional oven, bake at 350 degrees for 40 minutes.*

GARDEN AU GRATIN
Loni Holley, Holley Family Farms

olive oil

Yukon gold or red potatoes

zucchini

yellow summer squash

cheddar cheese, grated

fresh basil

garlic powder

salt and pepper

tomatoes

Note: This recipe does not contain exact amounts of ingredients. It can be adjusted to whatever is fresh picked from the garden or farmers market.

Preheat oven to 350 degrees. Spray 9"x13" or 8"x8" baking dish with olive oil. Slice potatoes thinly and place in casserole dish, about ¾-inch deep.

Slice zucchini thinly and layer over potatoes another ½- to ¾-inch deep. Slice yellow squash thinly and layer over zucchini another ½- to ¾-inch deep.

Splash olive oil over the top and sprinkle with garlic powder, salt, and pepper to taste.

Top with thick slices of fresh, ripe tomatoes. Sprinkle with cheese and basil. Bake uncovered for approximately 60 minutes, until vegetables are tender.

ZUCCHINI AND CHEESE BAKE
Bobbie Smith

1 small onion, chopped	½ teaspoon black pepper
1 ½ pounds zucchini, diced	1 ½ cups Monterey Jack cheese, grated
2 tablespoons butter	1 egg
1 (4-ounce) can diced mild green chiles	1 cup cottage cheese
3 tablespoons flour	2 tablespoons fresh parsley, chopped
½ teaspoon salt	½ cup grated Parmesan cheese

Preheat oven to 400 degrees. Sauté onion and zucchini in butter. Add chiles, flour, salt, and pepper. Pour into a greased casserole dish. Top with Monterey Jack cheese. Mix egg with cottage cheese and parsley; pour over zucchini mixture. Sprinkle with Parmesan. Bake for 25 to 30 minutes, until zucchini is tender and cheese is melted and bubbly. Serves 4.

• • •

LOST AND FOUND ZUCCHINI
Betty Phelan

8 cups diced zucchini	½ cup olive oil
1 green bell pepper, chopped	1 cup bread crumbs
1 large onion, finely chopped	1 teaspoon minced fresh basil
2 large eggs, beaten	1 cup grated sharp cheddar cheese

Note: This family recipe originally came from a newspaper article. The author reportedly misplaced it for several years and found it again. That is where the name "lost and found" came from.

Preheat oven to 350 degrees. In a large bowl, combine all of the ingredients. Oil the bottom of a 9"x13" baking dish, place the ingredients in it, and bake for 45 minutes or until the top is browned lightly. Serves 8.

SAUTÉED SUMMER VEGETABLES
Rae Vallem

Vegetables

2 medium yellow summer squash, sliced into ½-inch pieces

1 medium zucchini, sliced into ½-inch pieces

1 small red onion, cut into ½-inch wedges

1 cup green pepper, cut into ½-inch strips

½ sweet red pepper, cut into ½-inch strips

Marinade

¼ cup olive oil

2 tablespoons balsamic vinegar

1 tablespoon fresh lemon juice

2 garlic cloves, minced

½ teaspoon salt

½ teaspoon black pepper

⅛ to ½ teaspoon crushed red pepper flakes (optional)

Note: The most popular sweet pepper in the United States is the bell pepper.

Place vegetables in a large bowl. In a small bowl, whisk the oil, vinegar, lemon juice, garlic, salt, black pepper, and pepper flakes. Pour marinade over the vegetables; toss to coat. Cover and refrigerate for up to an hour. In a large skillet, sauté vegetable mixture for 3 to 6 minutes or until crisp-tender. Serves 4.

ZUCCHINI FRITTERS
John Kukulica

2 eggs

1 pound zucchini, grated

2 tablespoons chopped fresh parsley

1 clove garlic, minced

2 tablespoons lemon zest

¾ cup flour

¼ cup grated Parmesan cheese

salt and pepper, to taste

3 tablespoons olive oil for frying

Note: This is my wife Ghyslaine's recipe that we all enjoy. They are a hit at potlucks — guaranteed that people will be asking for the recipe!

In a measuring cup, beat eggs until blended. In a large bowl, combine zucchini, parsley, garlic, lemon zest, flour, Parmesan, salt and pepper. Mix well. Stir eggs into vegetable mixture.

Heat 3 tablespoons olive oil in a nonstick pan to medium-high heat. For each fritter, ladle about 1 ½ ounces of batter into the hot olive oil. Brown fritter on both sides (a couple of minutes on each side), and remove from pan. Drain on paper towels. Serve warm. Makes about 12 small fritters.

COLACHE
Loni Holley, Holley Family Farms

2 tablespoons olive oil

1 pound fresh green beans, trimmed and cut into 1-inch pieces

2 medium yellow onions, coarsely chopped

1 pound zucchini, cut into 1-inch cubes

1 pound yellow crookneck squash, cut into 1-inch cubes

4 large Anaheim chiles, peeled, seeded, deveined, and diced, or 1 (7-ounce) can diced green chiles

6 medium (2 cups) Roma tomatoes, peeled and coarsely chopped, or 1 (14-ounce) can diced tomatoes

2 cloves garlic, crushed

1 teaspoon salt

cut corn from 2 large ears fresh corn, previously cooked

1 teaspoon chopped fresh oregano, or ½-teaspoon dried oregano

½ pound extra-sharp cheddar cheese, shredded

Note: Skins are easy to remove from frozen tomatoes. They slide right off.

In a large heavy-bottomed pot, heat olive oil over medium-high heat. Add green beans and stir-fry until the skins start to blister. Add onions and continue to cook until translucent. Add zucchini, squash, and chiles; cook for a few minutes more.

Stir in tomatoes, garlic, and salt. Reduce heat to low and cook covered for 20 minutes. Do not stir. Add corn and oregano and cook for 5 minutes more. Top with cheese before serving. Serves 8.

CASHEW CHEESE PIZZA
Edita Sirusaite

Cashew cheese

1 cup raw cashews

3 cups water

1 clove garlic

¼ cup fresh lemon juice

1 tablespoon Dijon mustard

¼ cup water

½ cup fresh basil leaves

½ cup nutritional yeast

½ teaspoon onion powder

salt and pepper, to taste

Pizza

1 package of pre-made whole wheat pizza dough (or try making dough from scratch)

2 summer squash, sliced thinly

1 medium sweet onion, sliced thinly

8 ounces fresh mushrooms, sliced thinly

Note: When I started a vegan journey, I had to come up with recipes that my meat-and cheese-eating man would love. This pizza was a hit. We love it, and I hope you will too. Of course you can add meat, but trust me and try it without meat to enjoy the texture of the wonderful cashew cheese!

Soak cashews in 3 cups of water for at least one hour, up to 24 hours. The longer you soak them, the more creamy they will become. Drain and rinse soaked cashews.

Add cashews, garlic, lemon juice, mustard, ¼ cup water, basil, nutritional yeast, onion powder, salt, and pepper to a food processor and process until smooth.

Preheat oven to 450 degrees. Stretch pizza dough on pizza pan.

Preheat pan for sautéing. Add a little bit of water and add all veggies to the pan. Sauté veggies on medium low for a few minutes, until soft. Remove pan from the stove and let veggies cool for a few minutes.

Spread cashew cheese over pizza dough. Spread vegetables over cashew cheese.

Bake pizza for 12 minutes, until crust is browned. Enjoy!

GRILLED MARINATED FLANK STEAK
WITH CHIMICHURRI SAUCE
Chef Ann Wiles
Recipe made for Bently Ranch

Chimichurri sauce

1 ½ cups finely chopped flat-leaf parsley
(approximately 2 bunches, thick stems
trimmed away)

¼ cup finely chopped fresh basil

¼ cup finely chopped fresh oregano

zest and juice of 3 limes

splash of sherry vinegar

4 cloves garlic, minced

2 teaspoons crushed red pepper

kosher salt and freshly ground black
pepper, to taste

Marinated steak

1 flank steak, approximately 2 pounds

½ cup olive oil

½ cup soy sauce

½ cup honey

¼ cup red wine vinegar

1 teaspoon Dijon mustard

1 teaspoon freshly ground black pepper

kosher salt and freshly ground pepper,
to taste

Chimichurri sauce
Combine all ingredients and season with salt and pepper, to taste.

Marinated steak
Combine olive oil, soy sauce, honey, vinegar, mustard, and 1 teaspoon pepper in a
1-gallon Ziploc bag and mix well. Add flank steak. Marinate at least six hours: overnight
is best.

Get your grill hot. Remove flank steak from marinade and pat dry with paper towels.
Season with freshly ground black pepper and kosher salt, to taste. Lightly oil the grill
grates and place the flank steak over direct high heat.

Grill about 6 minutes per side for medium rare or longer, depending on how you like
it cooked. Remove from grill, tent loosely with foil, and rest 10 minutes before slicing
thinly across the grain. Serve with chimichurri sauce. Serves 8.

CRUSTLESS ZUCCHINI TOMATO QUICHE
Jennie Zielinski

Vegetable base	Topping
2 cups zucchini, chopped into ½-inch pieces	1 ½ cups milk
2 cups tomatoes, chopped	¼ cup flour
½ cup onion, chopped	½ cup medium-ground cornmeal
⅓ cup grated Parmesan cheese	1 teaspoon baking powder
	1 teaspoon salt
	½ teaspoon pepper
	3 eggs

Variations: Chop some of your favorite fresh herbs and add for extra flavor. In the spring or fall, substitute finely chopped broccoli, spinach, or kale for the zucchini and tomatoes.

Preheat oven to 350 degrees. Place zucchini, tomatoes, onion and cheese in a greased 10-inch pie pan or 2-quart casserole dish.

In a blender, beat milk, flour, cornmeal, baking powder, salt, pepper, and eggs until smooth (15 seconds or more). Pour over vegetables. Bake approximately 50 to 60 minutes, or until knife inserted in center comes out clean. Let stand a few minutes to cool before serving. Serves 8.

HASENPFEFFER
Sue Kennedy, Kennedy Ranch

1 (3-to 3 ½-pound) rabbit, cut into serving pieces

½ teaspoon kosher salt

½ teaspoon pepper

¾ cup all-purpose flour, divided

⅓ pound pork bacon, diced

4 large shallots, finely chopped

3 minced garlic cloves

1 ½ cups good dry red wine (such as a Cabernet or Petit Verdot)

1 ½ cups chicken stock

¼ cup good-quality bourbon/whiskey

1 tablespoon red raspberry preserves

1 fresh bay leaf

1 sprig fresh rosemary

2 sprigs fresh thyme

2 tablespoons softened butter

1 lemon, quartered

Note: Hasenpfeffer is a traditional German stew made with rabbit.

Rinse the rabbit pieces, then dry with paper towels. Season with salt and pepper. Put ½ cup of the flour in a large mixing bowl, dredge the rabbit pieces, and shake off the excess.

Cook the bacon over medium heat in a heavy-bottom pot or Dutch oven for 3 to 4 minutes as the fat renders. Add the shallots and garlic and cook a few more minutes, until the shallots are translucent. Use a slotted spoon to transfer the bacon, shallots, and garlic to a bowl.

Increase the heat to high and add the rabbit, a couple of pieces at a time. Using tongs, brown the rabbit on all sides. If not enough fat remains to brown all of the meat, add a high-heat oil such as virgin coconut oil. Lower the heat if the bacon fat gets too hot. Transfer the rabbit to a plate and finish cooking the other pieces. Drain off the bacon fat and any burnt bits, and pour in the wine and chicken stock. Simmer over low heat for 5 minutes. Stir in the bourbon, raspberry preserves, bay leaf, rosemary, and thyme. Put the rabbit and any accumulated juices in the pot, cover tightly, and simmer for 1 to 1 ½ hours, until well done. Transfer the rabbit to a serving platter and cover with aluminum foil. Strain the sauce and discard the solids.

Return the shallots, garlic, and bacon to the sauce in the pot and bring it to a simmer. Mix the softened butter into the remaining ¼ cup flour to make a paste. Whisk the flour paste into the sauce, until it thickens to a gravy consistency. Taste the sauce and add salt and pepper if needed. Remove the foil from the rabbit and squeeze lemon juice over the pieces. Spoon sauce over the rabbit, and serve extra sauce in a gravy boat. Serve with red cabbage, spaetzle, noodles, or mashed potatoes. Serves 4 to 6.

SHIRAZ SOY TRI-TIP
Loni Holley, Holley Family Farms

1 beef tri-tip (about 2 ½ pounds),
    fat trimmed, rinsed and patted dry

¾ cup Shiraz (Syrah) wine

⅔ cup soy sauce

¼ cup vegetable oil

¼ cup balsamic vinegar

¼ cup fresh lemon juice

2 tablespoons Worcestershire sauce

2 teaspoons Dijon mustard

1 ½ teaspoons minced garlic

Note: You can make extra marinade and use it to grill fresh vegetables such as peppers and onions. Cut vegetables into large slices and brush with marinade. Grill next to meat for about 15 minutes until tender, turning once. Do not use marinade from raw meat to grill vegetables, as you might contaminate the food.

Whisk together wine, soy sauce, oil, vinegar, lemon juice, Worcestershire sauce, mustard, and garlic. Place tri-tip in a glass bowl or plastic food-grade bag or container. Marinate for at least 2 hours, but overnight is even better. Turn meat several times while marinating. Cook over medium grill for about 35 minutes or to desired doneness.

PITA PORK
Loni Holley, Holley Family Farms

5- to 7-pound pork roast	12 pita-pocket breads
1 cup water	fresh tomatoes, sliced
2 to 3 bay leaves	1 avocado, sliced
12 peppercorns	1 red onion, thinly sliced
salt, to taste	1 (8-ounce) container sour cream

Note: This is an old family recipe that my mother made when I was a kid. It is perfect for a light summer meal when it's too hot to cook.

Place pork roast in electric slow cooker with one cup of water, bay leaves, peppercorns, and salt, to taste. Cook eight hours on low heat. When done, shred pork. Serve warm in pita-pocket bread with tomatoes, avocado, onion, and sour cream. Makes 12 sandwiches.

• • •

GINGER & GARLIC PAC CHOI STIR FRY
Marilyn Yamamoto, Cowboy Trail Farms

6 bunches pac choi	2 teaspoons chopped or grated ginger
2 tablespoons coconut oil	pinch of red pepper flakes
1 teaspoon sesame oil	1 tablespoon soy sauce
2 cloves garlic, chopped	1 tablespoon Hoisin sauce

Note: Pac choi, also known as bok choy, is a popular Chinese green, a member of the cabbage family, and a great source of vitamins A and C. If you can't find pac choi or bok choy, you can substitute with green kale or napa cabbage.

Wash and dry pac choi. Cut off ends, then cut into bite-size chunks (about 1-inch). Heat a saucepan or wok and add coconut and sesame oils. When oil is warmed, add garlic, ginger, and red pepper flakes and cook over medium heat for one minute.

Add soy sauce, Hoisin sauce, and pac choi. Stir until combined. Cook until pac choi is crisp-tender, about 3 to 5 minutes. If the pan becomes dry while cooking, add a tablespoon of water to steam it a bit. Serve with steamed rice.

PEPPERMILL SNOUT TO TAIL PIG PAELLA
Peppermill Casino Banquets

2 tablespoons olive oil

2 cups diced white onion

1 red or green bell pepper, diced

4 pounds hog offal and pig parts, large diced

8 ounces chorizo, large diced

4 cups chicken broth

1 cup diced roma tomatoes

3 garlic cloves

1 teaspoon saffron threads (crush after measuring — do not use too much, as it can ruin the flavor)

3 cups Arborio rice, uncooked

1 cup chopped parsley

1 cup green peas

½ cup fresh lemon juice

lemon wedges for garnish

1 teaspoon Spanish paprika

Note: Offal refers to parts of the animal that are used as food but aren't skeletal muscle. The term means "off fall," the pieces that fall from the carcass when it's butchered. It includes organ meats. Cooking with offal is more common in other countries, and it is making a comeback in the United States. You can get offal from your local hog farmer or butcher.

Heat olive oil in a large skillet on medium heat. Add onion, bell pepper, offal, pig parts, and chorizo. Cook until vegetables soften and proteins begin to caramelize.

Add broth, tomatoes, garlic, saffron, and rice. Turn heat to medium low and simmer for 5 minutes. Turn heat to low and cook for 20 minutes with lid on pan, until rice is barely cooked.

Add parsley, peas, and lemon juice to mixture and stir. Remove from heat and let rest for 10 minutes with the lid on. Sprinkle paprika over the top and serve with lemon wedges. Serves 8.

CROOKNECK SQUASH BREAD
Mary Manning

3 cups crookneck squash, grated (use a large squash with mature seeds for the best flavor)

1 cup brown sugar, firmly packed

½ cup honey

⅔ cup vegetable oil

2 teaspoons vanilla

4 large eggs

3 cups flour

2 teaspoons baking soda

1 teaspoon salt

1 teaspoon cinnamon

½ teaspoon ground cloves

½ teaspoon baking powder

seeds from the crookneck squash

Note: The seeds add a nice nutty flavor to the bread.

Preheat oven to 350 degrees. With shortening or cooking spray, grease the sides and bottoms of two 4"x8" loaf pans. In a large bowl, stir squash, sugar, honey, oil, vanilla, and eggs until well mixed. Stir in remaining dry ingredients except the seeds and blend well. Stir in seeds.

Divide batter evenly between pans. Bake for 45 to 55 minutes, until toothpick inserted in center comes out clean. Cool in pans on cooling rack for 10 minutes before removing. Makes two loaves.

PINEAPPLE ZUCCHINI BREAD
Norma Petersen

3 eggs

1 cup vegetable oil

2 cups sugar

2 teaspoons vanilla

3 cups flour

2 teaspoons baking soda

1 teaspoon salt

½ teaspoon baking powder

1 ½ teaspoons cinnamon

¾ teaspoon nutmeg

2 cups grated zucchini squash

1 (8 ¼-ounce) can crushed pineapple, drained

1 cup chopped nuts

1 cup raisins

Note: The eggshell may have as many as 17,000 tiny pores over its surface. Through them, the egg can absorb flavors and odors. Storing them in their cartons helps keep them fresh.

Preheat oven to 350 degrees. Grease and flour 2 loaf pans. In a large bowl, combine eggs, oil, sugar, and vanilla; beat until thick and foamy. In a separate bowl, combine flour, baking soda, salt, baking powder, cinnamon, and nutmeg. Add to egg mixture and beat until well blended. Fold in zucchini, pineapple, nuts, and raisins. Pour into prepared pans. Bake for 60 minutes, until toothpick inserted near center comes out clean. Makes 2 loves.

CHOCOLATE MILK FROZEN FUDGE POPS
Barbara Moser

1 cup white sugar	3 cups whole milk
½ cup cornstarch	2 cups half & half
¼ cup cocoa powder	2 tablespoons butter
1 teaspoon instant-coffee granules	2 teaspoons vanilla
½ teaspoon salt	

Note: The inspiration for these frozen fudge pops is Sand Hill Dairy in Fallon, one of two artisan dairies in Nevada. Their fresh whole milk is divine!

Combine sugar, cornstarch, cocoa powder, instant-coffee granules, salt, and milk along with half & half in a medium saucepan over medium heat. Bring to a simmer; do not let mixture boil. Stir until thick, about 3 minutes.

Remove from heat. Stir in butter and vanilla. Transfer to a heatproof bowl and let cool. Pour into molds and freeze until firm, about 4 hours. Serves 8.

BERRY GALETTE
Jack Jacobs, Jacobs Berry Farm

3 cups fresh raspberries or blackberries

2 tablespoons flour

2 to 3 tablespoons sugar (depending on the sweetness of the berries)

2 frozen or refrigerated pie crusts (better yet if you make from scratch)

cinnamon sugar, optional (mix ½ cup white sugar with 1 tablespoon cinnamon)

Note: One of our favorite recipes at the berry farm!

Preheat oven to 400 degrees. In a large bowl, mix berries, flour, and sugar. On ungreased cookie sheets, unroll pie crusts and flatten. Pinch together any cracks in the pastry so they don't leak.

Place half of the berry mix on each pie crust, leaving a 2-inch border around the edge.

Fold the edge up and partially over the filling, forming loose pleats. Repeat with the second crust. If desired, sprinkle with cinnamon sugar, to taste.

Bake until the filling is bubbling and the pastry is golden brown, about 25 minutes. Transfer to a wire rack and let cool slightly before serving. Makes 2 galettes.

FRESH BERRY CRISP
Virginia Leslein

---

6 cups blackberries or raspberries or a
combination of the two, fresh or frozen

¾ teaspoon ground cinnamon

½ to ¾ cup brown sugar, firmly packed,
depending on the sweetness of the fruit

½ cup all-purpose flour

1 cup old-fashioned oatmeal
(not quick-cooking oats)

⅓ cup butter, softened

1 teaspoon water

¼ teaspoon salt

Note: You can substitute almost any type of fruit in this recipe, depending on the season. Try it with apples, peaches, pears, or plums, or better yet, experiment with a combination of your favorites.

Preheat oven to 350 degrees. If using frozen berries, thaw and drain well in a colander. Arrange fruit in a greased 8"x8" pan. Lightly sprinkle fruit with cinnamon. Mix together (with your hands is the best way) brown sugar, flour, oatmeal, butter, water, and salt.

Sprinkle oatmeal mixture evenly over fruit. Bake until topping is golden brown and crisp and bubbling in the center, 30 to 45 minutes. Serve alone or, if desired, with whipped cream or ice cream. Serves 12.

FRUIT COBBLER
Ginger Johnson

½ cup butter, melted

1 cup flour

1 cup sugar

2 teaspoons baking powder

¼ teaspoon cinnamon

1 cup milk

1 egg

1 teaspoon vanilla

1 teaspoon almond extract

1 tablespoon bourbon, optional

3 to 4 cups fresh fruit (any combination of berries, sliced peaches, plums, or nectarines)

fresh whipped cream or ice cream (optional)

Note: This is not a super-sweet recipe, so you may want to add more sugar if you prefer. I add sugar based on the sweetness of the fruit.

Preheat oven to 350 degrees. Pour butter into 9"x13" baking pan. In a large mixing bowl, mix together the flour, sugar, baking powder, and cinnamon. Add milk, egg, vanilla, almond extract, and if desired, bourbon. Beat until just mixed.

Pour into baking pan on top of melted butter. Add fresh fruit evenly to cover the batter. Bake for approximately 50 minutes, until batter is baked and a light golden brown. Top with fresh whipped cream or ice cream if desired. Serve warm or cold. Serves 12.

CHOCOLATE ZUCCHINI CAKE
Smith Family Favorite

½ cup mayonnaise	4 tablespoons cocoa powder
½ cup canola oil	1 teaspoon baking soda
1 teaspoon vanilla	½ teaspoon baking powder
1 cup buttermilk	1 teaspoon salt
2 eggs	2 cups zucchini, finely grated and patted dry
2 ½ cups all-purpose flour	1 cup semi-sweet chocolate chips
1 ¾ cups sugar	1 cup chopped walnuts

Note: This is the recipe my family looks forward to most when the zucchini are ready to be picked every summer!

Preheat oven to 350 degrees. In a large mixing bowl, combine mayonnaise, oil, vanilla, buttermilk, and eggs. Mix well. In a second mixing bowl, stir together flour, sugar, cocoa powder, baking soda, baking powder, and salt.

Stir dry ingredients into wet ingredients to combine thoroughly. Fold in the zucchini until evenly distributed.

Pour batter into a greased and floured Bundt pan. Sprinkle the top of the batter with chocolate chips and walnuts.

Bake for about 45 minutes, until toothpick inserted near center of cake comes out clean. Cool cake for 15 minutes on a wire rack before removing from pan. Serves 12 to 16.

MAPLE ICE CREAM WITH BACON BRITTLE
Kelli Kelly, The Slanted Porch

Ice cream	Bacon brittle
3 egg yolks	3 strips bacon
¼ cup sugar	1 cup sugar
pinch of salt	1 tablespoon butter
1 cup whole milk	½ teaspoon baking soda
1 cup pure maple syrup	pinch of chili powder
2 cups heavy cream	

Note: This recipe was inspired by the fresh whole milk of Sand Hill Dairy, our artisan dairy in Fallon.

Whisk egg yolks, sugar, and salt until they are a pale yellow color. Pour mixture into a saucepan and whisk in milk, stirring over medium heat until almost simmering. Add the maple syrup and stir.

Refrigerate until cold. Stir cream into chilled mixture; churn in an ice-cream maker and transfer to airtight container. Freeze about 2 hours, until firm. Makes about 1 quart ice cream.

Cook bacon in a skillet over medium heat about 5 minutes on each side, or until crisp. Cool and drain bacon on paper towels and finely chop.

Heat 1 cup sugar in a saucepan over medium heat, stirring constantly for about 5 minutes or until it melts and turns golden. Remove from heat. Stir in butter, then baking soda, bacon and chili powder. Pour on to a buttered baking sheet and cool about 15 minutes, or until set.

Break two-thirds of the brittle into bite-sized pieces and smash the rest. Serve ice cream with bacon brittle sprinkled on top or place ingredients in a blender to make as a milk shake.

LAVENDER WHITE CHOCOLATE COOKIES
Diana Van Camp, Campie's Lavender Patch

2 cups flour

1 cup granulated sugar

1 teaspoon baking soda

1 tablespoon culinary lavender

½ teaspoon salt

1 cup white-chocolate chips

1 cup butter, room temperature

1 egg

1 teaspoon vanilla

Note: It's important to watch the baking time carefully. The center of the cookie should be almost done and the bottom of the cookie slightly brown. The secret to a perfect cookie is in the baking.

Preheat oven to 350 degrees. Mix flour, sugar, baking soda, lavender, salt, and white-chocolate chips in one bowl. Mix butter, egg, and vanilla in another bowl. Combine all ingredients from both bowls together. The dough should not be sticky. If it is, add 1 tablespoon of flour.

Drop dough by rounded spoonfuls on to cookie sheet. Bake for approximately 10 minutes. Remove to wire racks and cool. Makes 3 dozen cookies.

ZUCCHINI BARS
Tina Smith

Bars	Frosting
2 cups sugar	½ cup butter, softened
1 cup oil	¼ teaspoon almond extract
3 eggs	2 teaspoons vanilla
2 cups flour	2 ½ cups powdered sugar
1 teaspoon cinnamon	1 (3-ounce) package cream cheese
1 teaspoon salt	
2 teaspoons baking soda	
¼ teaspoon baking powder	
1 teaspoon vanilla	
2 cups grated zucchini	
¾ cup rolled oats (not instant)	
1 cup chopped nuts	

Note: Zucchini is a type of summer squash. Some people think they are two different things.

Preheat oven to 350 degrees. Grease and flour a 10"x15" jelly roll pan.

In a large bowl, combine sugar, oil, and eggs. Mix well. Add flour, cinnamon, salt, baking soda, baking powder, and vanilla. Combine thoroughly. Fold in zucchini, oats, and nuts. Spread evenly in prepared pan. Bake for 15 to 20 minutes, until toothpick inserted into center comes out clean. Cool in pan.

Mix together butter, almond extract, vanilla, powdered sugar, and cream cheese. Beat until well blended. Spread evenly over bars. Cut bars to desired size.

ZUCCHINI BREAD PUDDING
May Craig

4 pounds medium zucchini, approximately 6 to 8

2 tablespoons butter

¼ cup honey

1 ½ cups whole-grain bread cubes (approximately 3 slices)

2 eggs, slightly beaten

1 teaspoon vanilla

¼ teaspoon salt

½ teaspoon cinnamon

½ cup raisins

whipped cream (optional)

Note: Egg yolks are one of the few foods that naturally contain Vitamin D.

Preheat oven to 350 degrees. Grease an 8"x8" pan. Peel zucchini. Do not remove seeds or pulp. Cut in chunks. Purée in a food processor. Place puréed zucchini in a saucepan and over medium heat bring to the boiling point. Stir in butter and honey. Set aside.

Spread bread cubes evenly in bottom of the 8"x8" pan. Pour zucchini mixture over bread cubes. Combine eggs, vanilla, salt, cinnamon, and raisins; pour on top of zucchini mixture. Set in a shallow pan of hot water. Bake for 60 minutes, or until a toothpick inserted in the center comes out clean. Serve with a dollop of whipped cream, if desired. Serves 12.

FALL

GREEN VELVET SOUP
Julia Bledsoe

Ingredients	Garnishes
1 spaghetti squash, medium sized	Sriracha hot sauce
2 leeks with green tops	toasted pumpkin seeds
4 stalks celery	feta cheese, crumbled
1 large fennel bulb	cashew cream
2 tablespoons olive or coconut oil	chopped chicken breast
1 pound spinach leaves, coarsely chopped	crème fraîche
4 cups chicken or vegetable stock	
2 sprigs fresh tarragon (or 1 teaspoon dried)	
salt and pepper and seasoning blend such as Mrs. Dash Original, to taste	

Preheat oven to 350 degrees. Cut spaghetti squash in half. Place the halves, cut side down, in a large roasting pan or baking dish. Bake for about 45 minutes, until tender, or microwave on high for about 12 minutes. Allow to cool.

Remove seeds; scoop out squash and set aside. Chop the leeks, including most of the green tops. Chop the celery and fennel, including some of the fern-like tops if you like. Add oil to a 4-quart stock pot. Add the leeks, celery, and fennel, stirring to coat. Cover and sweat down on medium heat until translucent. Add spinach and 1 cup of stock.

Reduce heat and simmer for about 10 minutes, stirring if needed. When the spinach is completely wilted, add the remaining stock, spaghetti squash, tarragon, salt and pepper, and other seasoning. Using a stick blender, purée the ingredients until smooth. If too thick, add more stock to thin slightly. Garnish to taste. Serves 6.

CARAMELIZED ONION-POTATO SOUP
Shawn Uhland

8 ounces bacon, coarsely chopped

6 cups sliced onions

5 cloves garlic, minced

4 cups thinly sliced potatoes

6 cups chicken or vegetable broth

4 ounces ham, chopped

½ teaspoon salt

½ teaspoon pepper

2 tablespoons fresh dill or 1 tablespoon dried dill

½ cup sour cream

Note: Never store potatoes and onions next to each other. They both release moisture and gases that will cause the other to spoil faster. However, they taste great cooked together.

Cook bacon until brown and crisp. Remove and drain on paper towels, reserving drippings in pot. Add onions to pot. Cover and cook until wilted. Remove lid and continue to cook until golden brown.

Add garlic. Stir in potatoes. Add broth, ham, salt, and pepper. Bring to a boil. Cook until potatoes are tender. Add dill. Remove pan from heat and stir in sour cream. Serve topped with bacon. Serves 6.

EASY PUMPKIN SOUP
Norma Petersen

To prepare pumpkin

1 sugar pie pumpkin, about 4 pounds

salt and pepper

Soup

2 tablespoons olive oil

1 shallot, peeled and diced

2 cloves garlic, peeled and minced

1 to 1 ½ teaspoons salt

½ teaspoon black pepper

1 tablespoon minced fresh sage

2 cups roasted pumpkin flesh

3 cups chicken stock

½ cup cream

chives or sage leaves, for garnish

Note: For roasted pumpkin seeds, save the seeds. Rinse them free of strings, then dry. Toss with olive oil and seasonings. Spread on a baking sheet. Roast at 300 degrees until golden, about 35 to 45 minutes.

Preheat oven to 375 degrees. Thoroughly clean the exterior of the pumpkin.

Using a sharp knife, carefully cut the pumpkin in half. Scoop the cavity clean of seeds and stringy flesh. Season the insides of the pumpkin halves with salt and pepper.

Place the pumpkin halves cut side down in a large roasting pan or baking dish. Add enough water or chicken stock to the pan so the liquid reaches about an inch up the side of the pan. Roast the halves for about an hour, until fork tender.

After the pumpkin has cooled, scoop out the flesh and mash or purée in a food processor. A 4-pound sugar pie pumpkin will yield about 1 ½ to 2 cups of roasted flesh.

Add olive oil to a medium-sized soup pot. Add shallot and garlic; season with salt and pepper. Sauté over medium heat until veggies are translucent, about 8 minutes. Add sage and cook an additional 2 minutes. Add pumpkin and stir.

Mix in chicken stock and simmer for 15 to 20 minutes, until thickened. Remove from heat. Purée in food processor or blender. Pour soup back into pot and add cream. Cook over medium heat until soup is hot. Garnish with chives or sage leaves. Serves 4 to 6.

POTATO LEEK SOUP
Norma Petersen

3 large leeks (use only the white and pale-green parts)

2 tablespoons butter

salt and pepper, to taste

2 cups water

2 cups chicken broth (vegetable broth for vegetarian option)

2 pounds potatoes, peeled and diced into ½-inch pieces

marjoram, a dash

¼ cup chopped fresh parsley

2 teaspoons chopped fresh thyme or ½ teaspoon dried thyme

Tabasco sauce or other red chili sauce

Cut leeks lengthwise. Separate, clean, and chop. In a medium-sized sauce pan, cook leeks in butter with salt and pepper. Cover pan, cooking on low heat for 10 minutes, checking often. Do not brown leeks! Browning will give leeks a burnt taste.

Add water, broth, and potatoes. Bring to a low simmer and cook for 20 minutes. Scoop about half of the soup mixture into a blender. Purée and return to pan. Add marjoram, parsley, and thyme. Add a few dashes of chili sauce to taste. Add freshly ground pepper and 1 to 2 teaspoons of salt or more to taste. Serves 6.

AUTUMN HARVEST ANTIPASTO SALAD
Tiffany Dethmers

7 ounces rotini noodles (corkscrew pasta)

1 cup cauliflower tops, cut into bite-sized pieces

1 small yellow summer squash, chunked

1 small zucchini, chunked

¼ cup chopped fresh parsley

1 small coarsely chopped purple onion

2 teaspoons finely chopped fresh basil

1 ½ cups chunked Swiss cheese

1 cup grated Parmesan cheese

6 ounces salami, chunked

½ cup Kalamata olives, pitted and halved

½ cup olive or avocado oil

¼ cup white or red wine vinegar

1 teaspoon chopped fresh oregano

1 tablespoon ground pepper

2 cloves garlic, minced

Note: This recipe is perfect for any fall gathering: it's fresh, healthy, and always a delicious hit with guests! It has been passed down in our family for generations and is such a wonderful appetizer or side during the autumn months.

Cook and drain the pasta. Set aside to cool. In a large bowl, combine cauliflower, summer squash, zucchini, parsley, onion, and basil. Mix lightly.

Add cooled noodles, Swiss and Parmesan cheeses, salami, and olives. Mix again. In a measuring cup, mix oil, vinegar, oregano, pepper, and garlic. Stir into pasta mixture. Refrigerate leftovers; they will keep for one week if covered. Serves 8.

BUTTERNUT SQUASH SALAD
Arianne Smith

1 medium butternut squash	¾ teaspoon salt
3 tablespoons olive oil	½ teaspoon fresh orange zest
1 tablespoon red wine vinegar	⅓ cup finely chopped red onion
1 tablespoon fresh lemon juice	2 tablespoons chopped parsley
1 clove garlic, minced	¼ cup Parmesan cheese, grated (optional)

Preheat oven to 425 degrees. Lightly oil a large baking sheet. Peel and quarter squash. Remove seeds; cut crosswise into ¼ inch slices. Arrange squash slices in pan (they will overlap) and roast until tender, about 15 minutes. Set aside to cool.

In a small bowl, whisk together oil, vinegar, lemon juice, garlic, salt, and orange zest to make dressing. In a serving dish, layer squash slices, red onion, and parsley. Drizzle with dressing and top with Parmesan if you like. Serves 4.

• • •

GARLIC POTATOES
Eldon Louhela

2 pounds small red potatoes	½ cup chopped fresh parsley
½ cup olive oil	salt, to taste
2 heads of garlic, peeled and chopped fine (more or less, to taste)	

Note: Asparagus is a member of the lily family and is related to onions, leeks, and garlic.

Boil potatoes until tender. Leave skins on and dice into 1-inch cubes. In a large frying pan, sauté chopped garlic in olive oil over medium heat until tender and barely brown. Add parsley during the last minute or two. Stir potatoes into garlic mixture. Add salt to taste. Serves 6.

FALL HARVEST SALAD
Susan Emmons

Salad	Dressing
2 large sweet potatoes, peeled and cubed	¼ cup olive oil
2 tablespoons olive oil	2 tablespoons rice vinegar
¼ teaspoon salt	2 tablespoons orange juice
¼ teaspoon pepper	2 tablespoons pure maple syrup
2 cups cubed cooked turkey breast	1 tablespoon fresh lemon juice
2 medium apples, cubed	2 teaspoons minced fresh ginger root
1 cup chopped and toasted walnuts or pine nuts	¼ teaspoon salt
4 green onions, thinly chopped	¼ teaspoon ground nutmeg
½ cup minced fresh parsley	⅛ teaspoon pepper

Note: Nevada had 4,137 farms in 2012, according to the 2012 USDA Census of Agriculture.

Preheat oven to 400 degrees. Place cubed sweet potatoes in an ungreased shallow baking pan. Drizzle with oil and sprinkle with salt and pepper. Toss to coat. Bake for 25 to 30 minutes, until tender, turning occasionally. Cool to room temperature.

In a large bowl, combine the sweet potatoes, turkey, apples, nuts, green onions, and parsley. In a small bowl, whisk together all the dressing ingredients. Pour dressing over the sweet potato mixture and toss to coat. Serve immediately. Serves 6.

GERMAN POTATO SALAD WITH AN ITALIAN FLAIR
Tina Smith

---

2 pounds potatoes, scrubbed, halved, and sliced ¼-inch thick

¼ pound bacon, diced

1 clove garlic or shallot, minced

2 tablespoons olive oil

5 tablespoons red or white wine vinegar

1 teaspoon sugar

2 celery stalks, diced

¼ cup minced basil or parsley

salt and pepper, to taste

green onions (optional)

Note: Onions thrive in Nevada because of the dry climate.

Cook potatoes until tender. Drain, reserving ¼ cup of the liquid. Transfer the potatoes to a large mixing bowl and keep warm.

Meanwhile, cook bacon until crisp. Drain off all but 2 tablespoons of the bacon grease. Add crumbled bacon to potatoes. Add the garlic or shallot to the skillet and cook until slightly softened, about 3 minutes.

Stir in the reserved potato cooking liquid, oil, vinegar, and sugar. Bring to a boil. Pour the mixture over the potatoes and toss to coat. Add the celery, basil or parsley, salt, and pepper. Mix well. Top with finely sliced green onions if desired. Serve immediately. Serves 8.

JENNIE'S KRAUT AND CABBAGE
Jennie Zielinski

1 pound bacon

2 medium onions, chopped

1 medium cabbage, shredded or
  chopped fine

3 tablespoons cornstarch

1 (16-ounce) jar sauerkraut, drained,
  or 2 cups homemade sauerkraut

1 to 2 cups vegetable broth or water

dried dill weed (optional)

Note: This recipe is best served with Polish sausage or bratwurst.

Chop bacon into medium pieces and fry in large pan until crisp. Drain on paper towels. Pour off most of the bacon grease, reserving about 2 tablespoons for onions. Brown onions in bacon grease over medium heat until soft and golden brown, about 7 to 10 minutes. Set aside.

In a separate pan, steam cabbage in broth or water over medium heat until tender, about 7 to 10 minutes. Start with 1 cup of liquid to cabbage and add more if it begins to evaporate. Drain excess liquid from cabbage. Add bacon, onions, sauerkraut, and cornstarch to cooked cabbage. Add dill weed if desired. Cook over medium heat until warmed through and thickened. Serves 8.

HONEY-GLAZED CARROTS WITH FRESH MINT
Michelle Plummer

4 cups carrots, sliced into ½-inch thick rounds or sticks

2 tablespoons butter

1 ½ tablespoons honey

½ cup water

salt and pepper, to taste

1 to 2 tablespoons chopped fresh mint

Note: A hive of bees flies over 55,000 miles to bring you one pound of honey.

Combine carrots, butter, honey, and water in a skillet. Bring to simmer and cook until carrots are just tender and most of the liquid has reduced to a glaze, about 10 minutes. Season to taste with salt and pepper. Sprinkle chopped fresh mint on the carrots, toss well, and serve. Serves 4.

POTATOES WITH ROASTED GARLIC VINAIGRETTE
Norma Smith

3 tablespoons olive oil, divided

1 ¼ teaspoon salt, divided

½ teaspoon black pepper, divided

7 garlic cloves, with skins (unpeeled)

3 pounds medium red or gold potatoes, cut into quarters

3 tablespoons minced chives

2 tablespoons white wine vinegar

2 teaspoons Dijon mustard

Preheat oven to 400 degrees. Combine 1 ½ tablespoons olive oil, ½ teaspoon salt, ¼ teaspoon pepper, garlic, and potatoes in a roasting pan. Toss well to coat. Bake for 1 hour and 10 minutes, or until tender, stirring after 35 minutes. Cool 10 minutes. Squeeze garlic cloves to extract pulp. Discard skins.

Combine the garlic pulp with the remaining 1 ½ tablespoons olive oil, ¾ teaspoon salt, ¼ teaspoon pepper, chives, vinegar, and mustard in a large bowl. Stir well with a whisk. Add potatoes to bowl and toss well to coat. Serves 8.

GREEK-STYLE LEMON POTATOES
Erica Petersen

4 medium potatoes, sliced into ½-inch rounds (or 8 to 12 fingerlings, quartered)

¼ cup fresh lemon juice

1 tablespoon olive oil

1 ½ tablespoons chopped fresh oregano leaves or 2 teaspoons dried oregano

2 teaspoons lemon zest

3 cloves garlic

1 teaspoon salt

1 cup boiling water

⅔ cup crumbled feta cheese

Note: Most garlic in Nevada is used as seed garlic and shipped to California.

Preheat oven to 450 degrees and butter a 9"x13" baking dish.

In a large bowl, toss potato slices with lemon juice, olive oil, oregano, lemon zest, garlic, and salt. Layer the mixture in the baking dish.

Pour 1 cup of boiling water over the potatoes and bake, uncovered, until most of the water has evaporated and potatoes are tender, about 30 minutes.

Top with feta cheese and bake until golden, about 15 minutes more. Serves 4.

• • •

RED POTATOES WITH WILTED GREENS
Tammy Franklin

1 pound small red potatoes

2 tablespoons butter

2 tablespoons olive oil

2 cloves garlic, minced (or more to taste)

4 cups chopped kale or spinach

salt and pepper, to taste

Note: You can also add red chili flakes, shallots, bacon, or ham, to taste. If you're a garlic lover, don't be shy in this recipe!

Boil potatoes until tender. Drain and slice. Slightly brown potatoes in olive oil and butter. Add garlic. Cook until golden. Add greens and cook, covered, 3 minutes or until greens are wilted. Season with salt and pepper. Serves 4.

STUFFED BELL PEPPERS WITH CHILES

6 large red or yellow bell peppers (or a mix of the two)

¼ cup bread crumbs

¼ cup grated pepper jack cheese (or cheese of choice)

1 small jalapeño pepper, stemmed, seeded, and minced

1 small serrano pepper, stemmed, seeded, and minced

3 garlic cloves, peeled and minced

¼ cup minced yellow onion, or more, to taste

1 tablespoon olive oil

1 ½ pounds ground turkey

salt and freshly ground black pepper, to taste

1 small zucchini, diced

1 small yellow squash, diced

¼ cup pine nuts

½ pound tomatoes, diced

Note: As bell peppers mature, their color changes from green to red, and they become sweeter.

Preheat oven to 425 degrees. Clean peppers, slicing off tops, and remove core and seeds. In a bowl, combine bread crumbs and cheese. Set aside.

In a large skillet over medium heat, sauté jalapeño, serrano, garlic, and onion in olive oil for 2 to 3 minutes. Increase heat to medium-high and add ground turkey, salt, and pepper. Cook approximately 5 minutes, being careful not to overcook the turkey. Add zucchini and squash.

When meat is nearly done, add pine nuts and tomatoes, stirring all to combine. Remove from heat when done and place in a bowl to cool a bit. Using a large spoon, stuff peppers with turkey mixture. Arrange peppers in a casserole dish or loaf pan to keep upright.

Top with bread-crumb mixture. Cook 15 to 20 minutes, depending on how soft you prefer your peppers. Serves 6.

CHIMICHANGAS
Erica Smith

Meat

1 (5-pound) chuck or round beef roast

salt and pepper, to taste

Filling

3 tablespoons vegetable oil

3 cups finely chopped onion

¼ pound green chiles, chopped

1 (14-ounce) jar green-chile salsa

½ teaspoon garlic powder

¼ cup flour

¼ teaspoon salt

1 teaspoon ground cumin

Chimichangas

20 (8-inch) flour tortillas

oil for frying

Note: Optional toppings include guacamole, sour cream, shredded lettuce, diced tomato, sliced olives, chopped onion, and shredded cheese.

Meat

Place roast, salt, and pepper in a slow cooker on low for 8 to 12 hours. Meat should be fork-tender and pull apart easily. Allow to cool, removing any excess fat. Reserve cooking liquid. Shred meat with a fork and set aside. If you prefer, you can cook the roast in the oven. Place meat in a roasting pan and cover with foil. Bake in 250 degrees oven for 8 to 12 hours.

Filling

Heat oil in a large pot. Sauté onion and green chiles until tender. Add salsa, garlic powder, flour, salt, and cumin. Mix well.

Add shredded beef and mix all ingredients, adding a small amount of juice from the crock pot to allow mixture to stick together. Place about ½ cup of meat mixture in the center of each tortilla. Fold ends over the filling, and then fold the sides to center to make a packet. Repeat until all of the meat mixture is used.

Chimichangas

Heat oil in a skillet and fry 2 or 3 at a time, turning so both sides are golden brown, about 2 minutes per side. Drain on paper towels, then keep warm while frying remaining chimichangas. Serve with favorite toppings. Makes approximately 20.

BRUNSWICK STEW
Rae Vallem

2 cups diced fresh tomatoes

4 cups cubed potatoes

2 ⅓ cups chopped onion

2 cups chicken or beef broth

1 ½ cups cooked lima beans (you may substitute garbanzo, fava, or cannelloni beans)

1 ¼ cups chopped green bell pepper

1 cup sliced okra (needed for natural thickening; green beans or eggplant can be substituted, but flour or cornstarch will need to be added to thicken the stew)

1 cup barbecue sauce: smoked, spicy, sweet, your choice

½ cup chopped celery

½ teaspoon black pepper, or to taste

¼ teaspoon salt, or to taste

2 cups fresh corn, cut off the cob (about 3 ears) or 2 cups frozen corn

1 cup cooked and chopped chicken breast

¾ pound chopped smoked pork

Note: This is a traditional Southern dish, originally made with squirrel, opossum, or rabbit. It can be made with lamb, beef, chicken, venison, or pork. The trick to Brunswick stew is that it needs to be very thick, which may be attributed to the older tradition of cooking with game meats in cast-iron pots over open fires.

Place tomatoes in saucepan and simmer 10 minutes over low heat. Combine all ingredients in a 7-quart electric slow cooker. Cover and cook on low for 8 to 10 hours. Serves 8.

BURGUNDY BEEF STEW
Terry Bell, The Dutch Diva

2 ½ pounds good-quality beef chuck, cut into 1 ½ inch cubes

1 (750 ml) bottle good burgundy red wine

2 whole garlic cloves, smashed

3 bay leaves

2 cups all-purpose flour

1 tablespoon kosher salt

1 tablespoon freshly ground black pepper

4 tablespoons olive oil, divided

2 yellow onions, cut into 1-inch cubes

1 pound carrots, peeled and cut diagonally in 1 ½ inch chunks

½-pound white mushrooms, stems discarded and halved

1 pound small potatoes, halved or quartered

1 tablespoon minced garlic (3 cloves)

2 cups chicken stock or broth

1 large branch fresh rosemary

½ cup chopped sun-dried tomatoes

2 tablespoons Worcestershire sauce

salt, to taste

2 teaspoons pepper

1 cup frozen or fresh peas

Note: This recipe originated with my daughter Sarah, who is truly a gourmet cook and focuses on fresh, organic ingredients when cooking for her family. Marinating the meat overnight in a good burgundy wine gives this stew a robust, rich flavor that is enhanced by the fresh rosemary and sun-dried tomatoes. Serve with fresh biscuits or garlic mashed potatoes—yum!

Marinade

Place the beef in a bowl with red wine, garlic, and bay leaves. Place in the refrigerator and marinate overnight.

Combine the flour, 1 tablespoon salt, and pepper. Lift the beef out of the marinade with a slotted spoon and discard the bay leaves and garlic, saving the marinade. In batches, dredge the cubes of beef in the flour mixture and shake off the excess. Heat the olive oil in a large pot and brown half of the beef over medium heat for 5 to 7 minutes, turning to brown evenly.

Place the browned beef in a greased 12-inch Dutch oven. Continue to brown the remaining beef, adding oil as necessary. Place all the beef in the Dutch oven.

Heat another 2 tablespoons of oil in the large pot and add the onions, carrots, mushrooms, and potatoes. Cook for 10 minutes over medium heat, stirring occasionally. Add the garlic and cook for 2 more minutes.

Place all the vegetables in the Dutch oven over the beef. Add 2-½ cups of the reserved marinade to the empty pot. Cook over high heat to deglaze the bottom of the pan, scraping all the brown bits with a wooden spoon. Add the chicken stock, rosemary, sun-dried tomatoes, Worcestershire sauce, and 2 teaspoons salt and pepper, to taste.

Pour the sauce over the meat and bake at 350 degrees for 1 ½ to 2 hours, using approximately 14 pieces of charcoal on the bottom and 14 pieces of charcoal on the top, until the meat and vegetables are all tender, stirring once or twice during cooking. Before serving, stir in the frozen peas, season to taste, and serve hot. Serves 8.

Can also be cooked on the top of the stove on simmer.

BRAISED GOAT SHANKS
Joanna Drakos

---

4 goat shanks (about ¾-pound each)

1 tablespoon olive oil

salt and pepper, to taste

½ lb shallots, chopped

2 to 3 carrots, sliced

3 cloves garlic, minced

⅓ cup brandy

1 cup water

1 cup red wine

¾ cup Medjool dates, pitted and
   chopped fine

1 bay leaf

1 or 2 sprigs each fresh rosemary and
   thyme, tied together with kitchen twine

Preheat oven to 225 degrees. Heat a heavy-bottom Dutch oven on the stove top on medium-high heat. Salt and pepper goat shanks, to taste. Add olive oil to hot pan and add goat shanks. Brown on all sides.

When nicely browned, move shanks to a plate. Add shallots to pan; add a pinch of salt and cook until they are translucent. Add carrots, stirring occasionally for an additional 5 to 6 minutes. Add garlic and stir for 30 seconds. The intoxicating aroma released by the garlic is your cue to add the brandy, deglazing the pan as you scrape up the browned bits.

Allow the brandy to reduce until bubbling and almost evaporated. Add the water and wine and return to a boil. Add the chopped dates. Reduce heat to medium low; add the bay leaf and rosemary thyme bundle. Return the goat shanks to the pan, along with any accumulated juices from the plate.

Cover the pan and bake for 3 hours or until the meat shreds easily with a fork. The chopped dates will have completely dissolved at this point. Remove from oven and lift out meat and solids with a slotted spoon on to a platter. Tent with foil to keep warm. Discard herb bundle.

Place Dutch oven on medium heat on stove top. Cook remaining liquid for a few minutes, until reduced to desired thickness. Serve shanks and carrots over mashed potatoes, polenta, or creamy grits. Ladle thickened reduction over the shanks. Garnish with thyme or rosemary sprig. Serves 4.

KOREAN-STYLE BENTLY RANCH SHORT RIBS

Chef Steve Anderson, Mid-Mountain Lodge at Northstar California
Recipe made for Bently Ranch

Marinade

1 cup lite soy sauce

½ cup brown sugar

½ cup Syrah

1 cup cold water

8 cloves garlic, minced

2 tablespoons sambal chili paste (more if you want spicier)

Ribs

6 pounds beef short ribs

¼ cup olive oil

1 bunch celery, rough chopped

1 large yellow onion, rough chopped

3 large carrots, rough diced

6 chile de arbol peppers, rough chopped

8 cloves garlic, peeled

2 quarts good beef stock (enough to cover)

½ bottle Syrah (750 ml)

Note: Chef Steve prepares these with beef short ribs from nearby Bently Ranch.

Marinade

Combine soy sauce, brown sugar, Syrah, cold water, garlic, and sambal chili paste. Add short ribs and marinate for up to 24 hours in a covered container in refrigerator. Do not marinate in a metal container.

Ribs

Preheat oven to 300 degrees. Drain marinade from ribs and discard. Heat a heavy braising pan. Add oil, celery, onion, carrots, chile de arbol peppers, and garlic.

Sauté over medium-high heat until mixture begins to caramelize. Push to side of pan and sear short ribs bone up, until top is nicely caramelized.

Flip ribs bone down, distributing vegetables evenly. Add beef stock and Syrah. Cover tightly with foil and bake for 3 hours, until tender. Pull from liquid and serve.

Great side dishes for this are grilled baby bok choy, steamed jasmine rice, and pickled radishes and chiles. Serves 6.

BATTLEBORN BISON BURGER WITH
RED-ONION CHUTNEY AND CAMEMBERT CHEESE
Steve Tucker, Renown Health

Red-onion chutney	Bison burger
2 ounces olive oil	2 pounds ground bison
1 tablespoon minced garlic	3 ounces panko bread crumbs
2 red onions, thin julienne	1 ounce Worcestershire sauce
2 yellow onions, thin julienne	2 cloves garlic, minced
2 green bell peppers, thin julienne	½ teaspoon kosher salt
4 ounces white sugar	¼ teaspoon ground black pepper
3 ounces balsamic vinegar	8 brioche buns
	1 pound Camembert cheese

Red-onion chutney

Heat oil in pan and add garlic. Sauté until flavor begins to develop. Add onions and peppers. Sauté until tender. Add sugar and vinegar. Heat until vinegar reduces to a syrupy consistency. Set aside.

Bison Burger

In a bowl, combine all ingredients except buns and cheese. Mix well. Form into 8 patties. Place in hot broiler, and brown on each side for 10 minutes or until cooked through. Top each patty with 2 ounces red-onion chutney and 2 ounces Camembert cheese. Heat until cheese begins to melt. Place buns in broiler and toast. Place each bison patty on a bun. Serve immediately. Serves 8.

KAELY'S BRISKET
Christie Casey-Braun, Alpine Ranch

1 tablespoon garlic salt	5 pounds brisket
1 tablespoon celery salt	2 tablespoons Worcestershire sauce
1 tablespoon onion salt	pepper to taste

Note: You can serve this with potatoes and carrots like a roast, or you can add your favorite barbecue sauce and serve it on a roll. You can chop up the leftover brisket and sauté it with onions and bell peppers and serve on a tortilla with black beans, cheese, avocado, sour cream, and salsa...it is amazing! If I am going to add barbecue sauce, I will usually take out about ¼ of the brisket before I add the sauce and save it in the refrigerator so I can make tacos with it the next night. My friend Kaely from Texas gave me this recipe. Texans know how to cook brisket!

Mix together the three salts and rub all over the brisket. Sprinkle brisket with pepper and Worcestershire sauce. Wrap tightly in aluminum foil. Refrigerate overnight.

Next day
Preheat oven to 225 degrees. Leave the brisket in the foil but place on a baking sheet. Bake for about 7 hours. When you pull it out, it should look somewhat stringy and break apart. Serves 6 to 12, depending on how hearty the appetite and how much you save for leftovers.

DISH IT UP PORK WITH ONION APPLE JAM

Nancy Horn, Dish Café

Pork

4 pork chops or 1 (2-pound) pork loin

1 tablespoon Dijon mustard

1 tablespoon brown sugar

1 teaspoon kosher salt

1 teaspoon freshly ground black pepper

Jam

4 tablespoons butter

1 tablespoon olive oil

2 large onions, peeled and sliced into half moons

2 apples, washed, cored, and sliced

3 tablespoons apple cider vinegar

salt and freshly ground black pepper

To finish

2 tablespoons butter

1 tablespoon olive oil

Note: Pork is not a "white meat." It's a lighter-colored meat, but pigs are not designed to be lean. Local pork is higher in fat, has more flavor, and is more tender than that found in grocery stores. Local pork is more like the traditional, old-fashioned pork from the '60s and '70s.

Remove pork from the refrigerator and let stand at room temperature for at least 30 minutes. Rub with mustard, then sprinkle with brown sugar, salt, and pepper. Rub the seasonings into the meat.

While the pork sits, add butter and olive oil to a large skillet over medium-high heat. When the butter has melted, add the onions, stirring to coat. Cook, stirring occasionally, until the onions are softened and starting to brown.

Add the apples and stir, cooking until the apples start to soften and brown. Add the vinegar and season with salt and pepper. Cook another 5 minutes, until the vinegar is reduced a little and everything is a little saucy. Remove the pan from heat and reserve the onion-apple mixture in a bowl.

Do not clean the pan. You'll use it to cook the pork.

Set the pan over medium-high heat and melt butter with olive oil. Add the reserved pork. If you're using chops, set them in the pan, cooking about 6 minutes per side uncovered. If you're using a loin, brown on all sides, then cover and cook until the middle reaches at least 145 degrees using a meat thermometer.

Remove the pork to a warmed platter to rest. Add the onion-apple mixture to the pan for 1 minute over medium-high heat, stirring to pick up the browned bits and reheating the mixture. Arrange the pork chops or slice the loin thickly. Pour the onion apple mixture over the pork with the juices. Serve immediately. Serves 4.

BACON AND EGG BREAKFAST CASSEROLE
Susan Emmons

1 pound bacon

6 slices of Texas toast or any thickly
  sliced bread

6 large eggs, beaten

1 ¼ cups milk

2 teaspoons dry mustard

1 teaspoon dried minced onion

2 cups (8 ounces) grated mild
  cheddar cheese

jalapeños and bell peppers (optional)

Note: We usually make this for Christmas morning or if we have overnight visitors. We
always get compliments for this dish.

Cook bacon until crisp. Cool on paper
towels. Crumble the bacon. Place bread
in a lightly greased 9"x13" baking dish.
Set aside.

Combine eggs, milk, dry mustard, and
onion. Pour over the bread. Sprinkle
crumbled bacon over the egg mixture.
Cover and refrigerate at least 8 hours
or overnight.

Preheat oven to 350 degrees. Remove
casserole from the refrigerator and let
stand for 30 minutes. Bake covered for
20 to 25 minutes.

Uncover and sprinkle cheese over the
top. Bake for an additional 5 minutes or
until knife inserted in the center comes
out clean. Let casserole stand for 5 to 10
minutes before serving. Serves 6.

ROASTED CHICKEN WITH FALL VEGETABLES
Amber Chevalier

1 ½ pounds boneless chicken breast, cut into 1-inch pieces

poultry seasoning

salt & pepper

2 cups carrots, cut into thin slices

3 cups sweet potatoes, peeled and cut into ½-inch pieces

½ red onion, cut into 1-inch pieces

¾ cup maple syrup

2 tablespoons olive oil

2 tablespoons chopped fresh thyme

1 tablespoon chopped fresh rosemary, removed from stem

Note: Choose veggies from all color ranges, as each color represents a different set of nutrients.

Preheat oven to 350 degrees. In a medium bowl, sprinkle chicken with poultry seasoning; add salt and pepper to taste. Set aside. Oil the bottom of a 9"x13" baking dish and place carrots, sweet potatoes, and onions on the bottom.

Mix maple syrup and olive oil together and drizzle over vegetables. Add thyme and rosemary. Toss to coat. Cover with tin foil and bake for 25 minutes. Remove foil, and add chicken. Stir and cook an additional 20 to 25 minutes, until chicken is cooked through. Let stand 5 minutes before serving. Serves 6.

OPEN-FACED SUPER SLOPPY JOES
Jesse Alexander

½ pound lean ground beef

½ pound pork chorizo

2 tablespoons butter, softened

½ medium yellow onion, chopped

1 (4-ounce) can green chiles, chopped

½ bell pepper, chopped

½ cup amaranth greens, chopped

½ cup ketchup

1 (16-ounce) can tomato sauce

½ teaspoon Worcestershire sauce

⅛ teaspoon smoked paprika

⅛ teaspoon cumin

salt and pepper, to taste

jalapeño peppers, chopped, to taste (optional)

4 cheddar-cheese Kaiser rolls or sweet-onion hamburger buns, buttered and toasted

1 cup shredded pepper jack cheese

Note: If amaranth greens are not available, use fresh spinach.

Over medium-high heat, brown ground beef and chorizo in a large cast-iron skillet.

Remove from skillet and pat down with paper towel to remove some, but not all, of the fat. Set meat aside. Reduce heat to medium low and add butter.

When melted, add chopped onions and canned green chiles. Cook 5 minutes, until onion is translucent. Add chopped bell pepper. Cook for 3 more minutes.

Add chopped amaranth greens and cook for 1 more minute. Add beef and chorizo back to the pan, along with ketchup, tomato sauce, Worcestershire sauce, paprika, and cumin. Simmer for 10 minutes.

Season with salt and pepper, to taste. Add jalapeño peppers, if desired. Serve over toasted open-face buns or rolls. Top with shredded cheese. Serves 4.

SPICY HAWAIIAN RIBS
Tanner Zahrt

BBQ sauce

2 tablespoons grape-seed or canola oil

4 garlic cloves, smashed

1 large onion, chopped

3-inch piece fresh ginger, peeled and finely
chopped

3 cups fresh pineapple chunks

2 jalapeño peppers, chopped

1 cup fresh pineapple juice

2 cups hoisin sauce

¼ cup ketchup

¼ to ½ cup dark brown sugar (depending
on how ripe the pineapple is)

3 tablespoons chili powder

2 tablespoons mustard

2 tablespoons honey

2 tablespoons soy sauce

pinch of cloves

1 teaspoon ground cinnamon

salt and freshly ground black pepper

Rub

¼ cup paprika

1 ½ tablespoons dry mustard

1 tablespoon ground ginger

1 tablespoon ground star anise

1 ½ teaspoons ground allspice

1 ½ teaspoons kosher salt

1 ½ teaspoons ground black pepper

1 teaspoon chili flakes (optional–
if you like spicy)

Ribs

2 racks St. Louis-style pork ribs (or beef
ribs if you prefer)

canola oil (enough to lightly coat ribs)

2 cups pineapple juice

2 cups water

1 tablespoon Asian Five Spice

1 tablespoon Jamaican jerk spice

½ cup fresh ginger, peeled and chopped

6 garlic cloves, smashed

1 teaspoon liquid smoke

BBQ sauce

Heat the oil over medium heat in a heavy-bottomed pan. Add the garlic, onion, and ginger. Cook for about 5 minutes, until onions are soft. Add the pineapple chunks and jalapeño, cooking for one minute. Pour in the pineapple juice and let cook until it caramelizes. Add hoisin sauce, ketchup, brown sugar, chili powder, mustard, honey, soy sauce, cloves, cinnamon, salt, and pepper, to taste. Cook until thickened, about 30 minutes. Transfer to a blender and blend until smooth. Pour into a bowl and allow to cool.

Rub

Combine paprika, dry mustard, ground ginger, star anise, allspice, salt, pepper, and chili flakes in a bowl. Mix well.

Ribs

Trim the thin membrane from the back of the ribs. Coat the ribs lightly with canola oil. Rub the ribs with the dry rub and wrap in plastic. Let sit for a couple of hours or more: overnight is best.

Preheat oven to 325 degrees. Place a rack in the bottom of a large roasting pan. Pour the pineapple juice and water into the pan. Sprinkle the Asian Five Spice, jerk spice, ginger, garlic, and liquid smoke into the liquid. Remove plastic wrap from the ribs and place them on the rack. Pour a small amount of sauce on the ribs. Cover the pan in foil and bake for 2 to 3 hours. Check the ribs after 90 minutes and remove from the oven when the meat begins to fall off the bone. Cover the ribs in sauce and serve. Serves 4.

Optional: Place ribs on a preheated grill for a couple of minutes to get a nice char.

SLOW COOKER BEEF AND CABBAGE
WITH POTATOES AND CARROTS
Peri & Sons Farms

---

1 (2-pound) beef brisket, trimmed

1 ¾ teaspoons salt, divided

¾ teaspoon freshly ground black pepper, divided

2 tablespoons brown sugar

2 teaspoons ground mustard

1 teaspoon ground cinnamon

½ teaspoon ground ginger

¼ teaspoon ground cloves

1 cup unsalted beef stock

3 tablespoons cider vinegar

2 teaspoons Worcestershire sauce

3 medium onions, cut into wedges

4 garlic cloves, crushed

2 bay leaves

1 head Savoy cabbage, halved (or 1 small head of green cabbage)

2 pounds small red potatoes, cut in half

1 pound carrots, cut into 1-inch pieces

1 tablespoon unsalted butter, melted

Note: This recipe is a good alternative to store-bought corned beef, as it is much lower in sodium and doesn't have the sodium-nitrite preservative often found in pre-packaged corned beef.

Combine 1 ½ teaspoons of the salt, ½ teaspoon pepper, brown sugar, mustard, cinnamon, ginger, and cloves in a small bowl. Rub mixture over all sides of brisket.

Place brisket in a 6-quart slow cooker. Add stock, vinegar, Worcestershire sauce, onions, garlic, and bay leaves. Arrange cabbage halves over top. Cook on low temperature for 8 hours, until beef is very tender.

Transfer beef to a cutting board discarding bay leaves. Place potatoes and carrots in a large saucepan. Add cold water to cover potatoes by 1-inch. Bring to a boil and cook 8 to 10 minutes, until tender. Drain.

Toss with remaining ¼ teaspoon salt, ¼ teaspoon pepper, and butter. Cut brisket across the grain into thin slices. Cut each cabbage half into 4 wedges. Serve brisket with onions, cabbage, potatoes, carrots, and au jus. Serves 8.

SKILLET POTATO AND CABBAGE PANCAKES
Mary Pillard

1 cup shredded cabbage	1 ½ teaspoons salt
2 ½ cups grated potatoes	½ teaspoon black pepper
¼ cup sliced scallions or chopped onions	¼ cup butter
1 clove garlic, minced	2 tablespoons vegetable oil
1 egg, beaten	sour cream or applesauce (optional)

Note: Kohlrabi is often described as that alien-looking vegetable. It's about the size of a large turnip and has several stems sticking out. It is a member of the cabbage family and is delicious raw or cooked.

Place shredded cabbage in a steamer basket. Steam until tender, 15 to 20 minutes. Squeeze excess water out of potatoes (makes for crispier potato). Combine the potatoes, cabbage, garlic, egg, salt, and pepper in a bowl. Mix well. Use your hands to form thin, loose patties. Heat butter and oil in skillet. Cook patties until done to your liking, 7 to 10 minutes. Flip once while cooking. Top with sour cream or applesauce if you choose. Serves 4.

SPAGHETTI PIE
Michelle Plummer

6 ounces spaghetti	1 cup chopped fresh or canned tomatoes
2 tablespoons butter	1 (6-ounce) can tomato paste
2 eggs, beaten	1 teaspoon sugar
⅓ cup grated Parmesan cheese	1 teaspoon oregano
1 pound ground beef	salt and pepper, to taste
½ cup chopped onion	1 cup cottage cheese
2 minced garlic cloves	½ cup shredded mozzarella cheese

Note: Hamburger meat from a single steer can make about 720 quarter-pound hamburger patties in addition to other cuts of meat.

Preheat oven to 350 degrees. Cook spaghetti al dente and drain. Stir butter, eggs, and Parmesan cheese into hot spaghetti. Press spaghetti mixture into a buttered 10-inch pie plate, pressing into bottoms and up the side. In a skillet, cook ground beef, garlic, and onions until brown. Drain fat and stir in tomato paste, tomatoes, sugar, oregano, salt, and pepper. Spread cottage cheese over bottom of spaghetti crust. Fill pie with meat mixture. Top with mozzarella cheese and bake uncovered for 20 to 30 minutes, until heated thoroughly and browned on top. Serves 6.

SLOW COOKER PORK AND BEEF BOLOGNESE
Courtney Barnes

1 pound ground pork

1 pound ground beef

1 tablespoon olive oil

2 ½ teaspoons salt, divided

1 teaspoon black pepper, divided

1 medium onion, diced

1 cup carrots, diced

3 cloves garlic, minced

1 tablespoon dried basil

1 tablespoon dried parsley

1 (6-ounce) can tomato paste

7 cups tomatoes, peeled and chopped

1 cup beef stock

1 cup Cabernet or a fuller-bodied red wine

¾ cup heavy cream

Note: If using whole tomatoes from the freezer, defrost, peel (they will slip right off), and crush by hand, enough to yield 7 cups.

In a large skillet, brown ground pork in olive oil over medium heat, seasoning with ½ teaspoon salt and ½ teaspoon black pepper, cook 4 to 5 minutes. Remove pork from skillet.

In the same skillet, brown ground beef (add a bit more oil, if needed), seasoning with ½ teaspoon salt and ½ teaspoon black pepper, cook 4 to 5 minutes. Add cooked ground meats to slow cooker and turn on to low setting. Add onion, carrots, garlic, basil, and parsley.

Season with remaining 1 ½ teaspoons salt. Add tomato paste and mix well. Add crushed whole tomatoes to slow cooker. Stir in beef stock and red wine. Mix well. Let sauce cook on low for 8 hours.

When the sauce has half an hour left, stir in cream. Ladle the Bolognese over white or whole-wheat pasta—the nuttiness of whole wheat goes especially nice with the sauce—or even brown rice. Makes about 10 cups of sauce.

PUMPKIN BLUEBERRY MUFFINS
Ann Louhela

---

2 cups whole-wheat flour

1 cup old-fashioned rolled oats

3 teaspoons baking powder

½ teaspoon baking soda

½ teaspoon salt

1 teaspoon ground cinnamon

½ teaspoon ground ginger

¼ teaspoon ground cloves

¼ teaspoon ground nutmeg

1 cup buttermilk (or plain yogurt)

1 ½ cups pumpkin purée, homemade

¼ cup granulated sugar

½ cup packed brown sugar

⅓ cup canola or vegetable oil

1 egg

2 teaspoons vanilla extract

1 ½ cups fresh or frozen blueberries

Note: Pumpkin and blueberries are a tasty combination!

Preheat oven to 400 degrees. Line a standard 12-muffin tin with paper liners or grease the muffin tin.

In a large bowl, mix the flour, oats, baking powder, baking soda, salt, cinnamon, ginger, cloves, and nutmeg.

In a medium bowl, whisk together the buttermilk, pumpkin, granulated sugar, brown sugar, oil, egg, and vanilla.

Add the wet ingredients to the dry ingredients, whisking just until the ingredients are incorporated.

Gently stir in blueberries. Divide batter between the 12 muffin cups. Bake for about 15 to 18 minutes, until a toothpick inserted into the center of one of the muffins comes out clean.

HONEY BARS
Debbie Gilmore, Hall's Honey

½ cup butter, room temperature	½ teaspoon baking powder
½ cup sugar	¼ teaspoon salt
½ cup honey	1 cup quick-cooking oats
1 egg, beaten	1 cup coconut
⅔ cup flour	1 teaspoon vanilla
½ teaspoon baking soda	½ cup chopped walnuts

Note: In one day, a honeybee can fly 12 miles and pollinate up to 10,000 flowers.

Preheat oven to 350 degrees. Grease a 9"x13" baking pan. Cream butter, sugar, and honey until light and fluffy. Add egg and blend. Sift flour with baking soda, baking powder, and salt. Add to the creamed mixture. Stir in oats, coconut, vanilla, and nuts. Spread in prepared pan. Bake for 20 to 30 minutes, until light brown. When cool, cut into bars. Makes about 36 bars.

• • •

HONEY APPLE NUT RAISIN PIE
Leonard Joy, Joy's Honey Ranch

2 uncooked pastries for 9-inch pie crust (homemade or store-bought)	5 cups cored, peeled, and thinly sliced tart apples
⅓ cup packed brown sugar	½ cup raisins
¼ cup all-purpose flour	½ cup chopped walnut halves
½ teaspoon ground nutmeg	⅓ cup honey
1 teaspoon ground cinnamon	1 tablespoon butter
dash of salt	

Preheat oven to 425 degrees. Place bottom crust in pie pan. In bowl, mix sugar, flour, nutmeg, cinnamon, and salt. Toss with apples, raisins, and walnuts. Drizzle honey (warm slightly if needed to make it more fluid) over apples. Stir and turn apple mixture into pie pan. Dot butter over top. Place slit-top crust on, sealing and fluting edges. Bake 40 to 50 minutes, until crust is brown and juice begins to bubble through slits. Serves 8.

APPLE DATE BREAD
Hazel Gomes

1 (8-ounce) package pitted dates, chopped

1 cup raisins

1 cup apples, peeled and chopped into
¼-inch pieces

1 ½ cups boiling water

1 cup all-purpose flour

1 cup whole-wheat flour

1 teaspoon baking soda

1 teaspoon baking powder

¼ teaspoon salt

2 eggs, slightly beaten

1 teaspoon vanilla

⅓ cup unsweetened applesauce

½ cup chopped nuts (almonds, pecans,
or walnuts)

Note: The dates, raisins, and apples make this a naturally sweet recipe—no need to add extra sugar or oil.

Preheat oven to 350 degrees. Lightly oil a bread pan.

In a medium bowl, combine dates, raisins, apples, and boiling water. Set aside and cool for 10 minutes.

In a large mixing bowl, stir the flours, baking soda, baking powder, and salt. Set aside. Stir eggs, vanilla, and applesauce into cooled date mixture.

Add date mixture and nuts to flour mixture. Stir until well blended. Mixture will be thick. Spread evenly in prepared pan.

Bake for 40 to 50 minutes, until a wooden toothpick inserted in center comes out clean. Cool in pan for 10 minutes.

Remove from pan and cool thoroughly on a wire rack. Wrap and store overnight before serving. Makes 1 loaf.

MOCHA HONEY MOUSSE PIE
Chris Foster, Hidden Valley Honey

Crust

2 packages graham crackers
  (about 9-½ ounces)

¾ cup butter, melted

½ cup granulated sugar

Mousse

8 eggs, separated

1 envelope unflavored gelatin

¼ cup cold water

4 ounces cold espresso

2 cups semi-sweet chocolate chips

½ teaspoon cream of tartar

½ cup local honey, heated

2 cups heavy whipping cream

Crust

Preheat oven to 325 degrees. In bowl of food processor, add graham crackers and pulse until finely crushed. With blade spinning, slowly drizzle melted butter into graham-cracker crumbs until mixture holds together, adding sugar at the end. Press graham-cracker mixture evenly in the bottom of a 9 ½" springform pan. Bake for 10 minutes. Cool crust in pan.

Mousse

Separate eggs into two small bowls, one for the whites and one for the yolks. Dissolve gelatin in ¼ cup cold water in a separate bowl. In a double-boiler over simmering water, whisk the egg yolks with the cooled espresso and cook until mixture coats the back of a spoon. Drizzle in the dissolved gelatin, then add chocolate chips. Continue whisking until mixture is well blended. Remove from heat and cool (to 100 degrees).

In large bowl of stand mixer, beat egg whites with cream of tartar just until stiff peaks form. Warm honey in microwave until very hot, being careful not to boil. With beaters on, slowly pour hot honey into egg whites until just mixed. Meringue will be glossy.

In a clean, chilled mixing bowl and with clean beaters, whip cream on high until stiff peaks form.

In a very large bowl, pour in chocolate mixture, ⅓ of the meringue and ⅓ of the whipping cream. Whisk thoroughly. Gently fold in half of the remaining meringue and whipped cream, alternating. Finally, fold in the last of the meringue and whipped cream. Mousse may have streaks of white, but do not over mix, to keep the texture light. Pour mousse into cooled crust and refrigerate overnight. Serves 8 to 12.

SPICED CARROT MUFFINS
Amanda Gaffaney

¾ cup all-purpose flour	¼ cup butter, melted
1 cup whole-wheat flour	1 cup plain yogurt
½ cup brown sugar, packed	½ cup milk
1 ½ teaspoons cinnamon	2 large eggs
½ teaspoon nutmeg	2 cups carrots, peeled and shredded (about 5 medium)
¼ teaspoon ground cloves	1 cup raisins (optional)
2 teaspoons baking powder	1 cup chopped walnuts or pecans (optional)
1 ½ teaspoons baking soda	
½ teaspoon salt	

Note: Purple carrots were the norm until the 17th century, when Dutch growers developed the orange variety that is most popular today.

Preheat oven to 375 degrees. Line standard muffin cups with 18 paper liners; set aside.

In a large bowl, stir together flours, sugar, cinnamon, nutmeg, cloves, baking powder, baking soda, and salt; set aside. Melt butter in a small bowl in the microwave.

Whisk together yogurt, milk, and eggs. Add slowly to melted butter to avoid curdling. Make a well in the center of the dry ingredients and add yogurt mixture.

Stir until just combined—if it seems too dry, add more milk, one tablespoon at a time.

Fold in shredded carrots and optional raisins and nuts. Fill muffin cups two-thirds full. Bake for 15 to 17 minutes, until a toothpick inserted into center of a muffin comes out clean. Transfer to a wire rack. Serve warm or at room temperature. Makes 18 muffins.

HONEY OATMEAL BARS
Jennie Zielinski

2 cups old-fashioned oatmeal	1 teaspoon vanilla
½ cup chopped almonds	½ teaspoon salt
⅔ cup peanut butter	1 cup rice cereal, such as Rice Krispies
½ cup honey	⅓ cup dried fruit, your choice

Note: Good for breakfast or dessert: not too sweet and has a little protein.

Preheat oven to 350 degrees. Combine oatmeal and almonds. Bake in a single layer on a cookie sheet for approximately 15 to 20 minutes, stirring after 7 minutes, until lightly toasted. Do not let them get dark.

Heat the peanut butter, honey, vanilla, and salt in a saucepan on low heat until smooth.

Combine the oatmeal mixture with the rice cereal and dried fruit in a large bowl; stir well.

Pour hot peanut butter mixture over the dry ingredients and mix well. Pat the mixture into a lightly greased 8"x8" pan. Cool before serving.

SOFT PUMPKIN CHOCOLATE CHIP COOKIES
Natalie Andelin, Andelin Family Farm

1 cup brown sugar, packed	¼ teaspoon ginger
1 cup butter, room temperature	¼ teaspoon ground cloves
2 eggs	1 teaspoon cinnamon
1 ½ cups homemade pumpkin purée from 1 small sugar pumpkin	½ teaspoon nutmeg
2 cups flour	1 (12-ounce) package chocolate chips (milk, semisweet, or dark)
1 teaspoon baking soda	1 cup coarsely chopped nuts (walnuts or pecans)
1 teaspoon salt	

Note: This is a soft, moist cookie. It's delicious with or without chocolate chips!

Pumpkin purée

Preheat oven to 350 degrees. Cut a small pie pumpkin in half and scoop out the seeds. Bake halves on a baking sheet at 350 degrees for 45 to 50 minutes, until very soft when poked with a fork. When pumpkin is cool, scoop the flesh off the skin. It should come off easily. Mash the scooped flesh with a potato masher or pulse in a food processor.

One small pumpkin will make about 2 cups of purée. Extra purée may be stored in portions in the freezer.

Pumpkin Cookies

Cream butter and sugar. Add eggs and pumpkin and mix thoroughly. In a separate bowl, mix flour, baking soda, salt, ginger, cloves, cinnamon, and nutmeg. Add dry ingredients to the pumpkin mixture; mix well.

Stir in chocolate chips and nuts. Spoon onto ungreased cookie sheet and bake for 10 to12 minutes. Makes approximately 48 cookies.

WINTER

BUTTERNUT SQUASH BISQUE
Eldon Louhela

4 cups butternut squash, peeled and cut into 1-inch cubes

½ cup orange juice

⅓ cup brown sugar, packed

1 cinnamon stick

1 cup sliced leeks, white portion only

1 yellow apple, peeled and chopped

½ cup onion, chopped

¼ cup butter

4 cups chicken broth

⅓ cup whipping cream

salt and pepper, to taste

Note: If cinnamon stick is not available, substitute ¼ teaspoon ground cinnamon. If leeks are not available, substitute green onions.

Preheat oven to 450 degrees. In a roasting pan, toss squash cubes, orange juice, and brown sugar; add cinnamon. Cover and bake for 30 to 40 minutes, until squash is tender. Discard cinnamon stick; drain squash and set aside.

In a large saucepan, sauté leeks, apple, and onion in butter until tender. Add broth and bring to a boil. Stir in cooked squash and cook for 5 minutes. Add cream, salt, and pepper; heat through. Cool slightly.

In a blender, process soup in batches until smooth. Return all to the pan and heat through. Do not boil. Serves 8.

ROASTED WINTER SQUASH JALAPEÑO GINGER SOUP
Shelley Brant

2 medium butternut or other winter squash, approximately 4 pounds	1 teaspoon salt
	¼ teaspoon cayenne
8 tablespoons butter	3 cups chicken broth
8 tablespoons brown sugar	1 tablespoon brown sugar
2 tablespoons olive oil	3 cups water
6 cloves garlic, chopped	3 tablespoons heavy whipping cream
2 tablespoons peeled and grated ginger	crème fraiche (optional)
1 jalapeño chile, roasted, seeded and chopped (test chile heat and adjust to taste)	

Note: Butternut or buttercup are good varieties of winter squash for this soup.

Preheat oven to 400 degrees. Halve winter squash and remove seeds from cavity. Divide butter and brown sugar evenly and place in each squash half. Roast for 40 to 50 minutes, until flesh is tender. Cool and scoop out flesh.

Heat olive oil in a 4- or 5-quart pot over high heat. Add garlic, ginger, jalapeño, and salt. Cook, stirring constantly, until fragrant but not yet browned, 1 to 2 minutes. Add cayenne and cook, stirring for 30 seconds.

Add squash, broth, brown sugar, and water. Bring to a boil, lower heat to a simmer, and cook, stirring occasionally, until flavors meld, about 25 minutes or until tender.

In a blender or food processor, purée the soup in batches until smooth, then pour back into the pot. Add more liquid as necessary. Stir in cream and adjust seasonings to taste. Serve hot, with a swirl of crème fraiche if you like. Serves 8.

CURRIED BUTTERNUT SQUASH SOUP
Josh Codding, Yosh's Unique Deli

2 medium butternut squash, peeled and cut into one-inch cubes

2 tablespoons coconut oil, divided

1 tablespoon each of toasted cumin, coriander, and fennel seeds

2 yellow onions, rough chopped

2 celery sticks, rough chopped

4 carrots, peeled and rough chopped

10 cloves of garlic, chopped

1 serrano pepper, seeded and chopped

1 red bell pepper, seeded and chopped

1 tablespoon kosher salt

1 tablespoon garam masala

1 tablespoon curry powder

1 teaspoon pepper

2 to 3 quarts low-sodium vegetable stock

2 (14-ounce) cans coconut milk

pinch nutmeg

salt and pepper to taste

1 tablespoon apple-cider vinegar

Preheat oven to 350 degrees. Place cubed squash in a baking pan with 1 tablespoon of the coconut oil. Roast covered until fork tender, about 30 minutes.

Meanwhile, toast the cumin, coriander, and fennel seeds with the rest of the coconut oil in a stockpot over medium heat. Toast until fragrant and seeds are a rust color. Add the onions and sauté until translucent. Add the celery and carrots and sauté for 3 minutes.

Next, add the garlic and both peppers. Cook until the garlic becomes fragrant, about 2 minutes. Add salt, garam masala, curry powder, pepper, 2 quarts of the vegetable stock, and roasted squash.

Bring to a boil and simmer until the carrots are soft enough to purée. Add the coconut milk and purée all ingredients. Add more stock if the soup is too thick. Adjust flavor with salt, pepper, and nutmeg. Add apple-cider vinegar and serve. Serves 8 to 10.

KALE SALAD
Mark Estee, Campo

Salad	Dressing
10 cups kale, julienne cut	1 ½ ounces fresh lemon juice
kosher salt, to taste	1 ½ ounces champagne vinegar
fresh pepper, to taste	4 ounces grape-seed oil
1 cup grated Parmesan cheese for crumble	4 ounces extra-virgin olive oil
	2 tablespoons chopped garlic
	kosher salt, to taste
	fresh ground black pepper, to taste

Note: Nevada is the second major garlic-producing state. California is the first.

Preheat oven to 300 degrees. Line a cookie sheet with parchment paper. Sprinkle with grated Parmesan cheese to form a thin layer of cheese. Bake until cheese melts and browns, approximately 20 to 25 minutes; watch carefully. Remove from oven and let cool. Break into small pieces and set aside.

In a large bowl, toss the kale, salt, and pepper. Set aside. Mix all of the dressing ingredients in a bowl and whisk. Add dressing to the kale mixture and toss well. Add the Parmesan crumble and toss again. Serves 6.

ROASTED ONION SALAD

Roasted onions

2 large onions, peeled and cut into
 ½-inch slices

¼ cup plus ½ teaspoon olive oil, divided

4 cloves garlic, unpeeled

Dressing

2 tablespoons red wine vinegar

2 shallots, peeled and quartered

2 teaspoons minced fresh parsley

½ teaspoon crushed red pepper flakes

⅔ cup olive oil

salt and freshly ground black pepper, to
taste

Salad assembly

8 cups mixed salad greens

1 cup crumbled blue cheese

½ cup chopped walnuts, toasted

Preheat oven to 400 degrees. Place onions on a baking sheet and drizzle with ¼ cup olive oil, tossing to coat. Place garlic on a double thickness of aluminum foil and drizzle with remaining ½ teaspoon olive oil, tossing to coat. Wrap foil around garlic and place packet on the sheet with the onions.

Bake for 40 to 45 minutes, until onions are lightly browned and garlic is tender, turning occasionally. Remove onions and unwrapped garlic to another sheet pan and cool for 15 minutes.

Place vinegar and shallots in a blender. Squeeze softened and cooled garlic cloves from their skins into blender. Cover and pulse until blended. Add parsley and pepper flakes. Cover and process, gradually adding oil in a steady stream until combined. Season to taste with salt and pepper. If not using dressing right away, cover and refrigerate. Pulse or whisk dressing to recombine just before using.

In a large salad bowl, mix greens, blue cheese, and walnuts. Drizzle lightly with dressing and toss to combine. Taste, then add more dressing a bit at a time until desired taste is achieved. Divide salad among 6 to 8 bowls and top each serving with roasted onion slices. Serves 6 to 8.

ACORN SQUASH WITH CRANBERRY STUFFING
Tina Smith

---

2 acorn squash

¼ cup chopped celery

2 tablespoons chopped onion

2 tablespoons butter

1 apple, peeled, cored, and diced

½ teaspoon salt

⅓ teaspoon lemon juice

⅛ teaspoon black pepper

1 cup cranberries, fresh or thawed frozen

½ cup sugar

2 tablespoons water

Note: Winter squash is often interchangeable with pumpkin in recipes.

Preheat oven to 375 degrees. Cut squash in half; discard seeds. Cut a thin slice from the bottoms of squash halves so they sit flat. Place squash hollow-side down in an ungreased 9"x13" baking dish. Add ½-inch of water to dish. Cover and bake for 45 minutes.

Meanwhile, in a small skillet, sauté celery and onion in butter over medium heat until tender. Add apple, salt, lemon juice, and pepper.

Cook uncovered over medium-low heat until apple is tender, stirring occasionally.

Stir in cranberries, sugar, and 2 tablespoons water. Cook and stir until berries pop and liquid is syrupy. Turn baked squash halves over and fill with cranberry stuffing. Cover, then bake 10 to 15 minutes more, until squash reaches desired tenderness. Serves 4.

CIDER-ROASTED WINTER SQUASH
Jennifer Hobart

¼ cup apple juice or fresh apple cider

2 tablespoons cider vinegar

3 tablespoons olive oil

3 tablespoons butter, melted

4 pounds winter squash (butternut, acorn, etc.), peeled, seeded, and chopped into 1-inch chunks

4 sprigs fresh sage leaves, chopped

4 sprigs fresh thyme leaves, chopped

salt and pepper, to taste

Note: To make peeling and cavity-cleaning easier, use a knife to prick the squash in several spots, then microwave a few minutes for a small squash, about 10 minutes for a larger one.

Preheat oven to 400 degrees. Whisk together apple juice or cider, vinegar, oil, and melted butter in a large bowl. Add squash, sage, thyme, salt, and pepper. Toss to coat. Place squash in a single layer in a shallow baking pan and roast for 50 to 55 minutes, turning once, until tender and light golden brown around the edges. Serves 8.

RANCH POTATOES
Susan Emmons

6 to 8 medium potatoes,
    peeled and cubed

½ cup sour cream

1 cup ranch dressing

Note: My kids loved this dish as they were growing up. It is easy to put together and a great side dish for any meat meal.

Preheat oven to 350 degrees. Stir together the sour cream and ranch dressing. Thoroughly coat all potato pieces. Spread on a baking sheet and bake for 40 to 50 minutes, until tender. Turn after 20 minutes. Serves 5 to 6.

• • •

ITALIAN POT ROAST
Hazel Gomes

4-pound beef chuck roast

1 (8-ounce) can tomato sauce

8 ounces fresh mushrooms, sliced

4 cloves garlic, finely minced
    (or more to taste)

1 cup pitted black olives, drained and
    halved

½ teaspoon black pepper

3 beef-bouillon cubes

½ cup water

Note: This recipe makes a generous amount of juice, which can be used to make delicious French-dip-style sandwiches with leftover roast, olives, and mushrooms.

Place roast in slow cooker. Combine remaining ingredients and pour over roast. Cover tightly and cook on low heat for 10 to 12 hours or on high heat for 5 to 6 hours. Serves 8.

ALWAYS-TENDER YANKEE POT ROAST
Charley Leslein

3- to 4-pound beef arm or chuck roast	2 cups beef stock or beef bouillon
2 cloves garlic, minced	1 medium onion, chopped
¼ cup olive oil	2 to 3 carrots, cut into 1-inch chunks
salt and pepper, to taste	4 to 5 medium potatoes, cut into strips

Note: Nevada farms grow several varieties of specialty potatoes including fingerlings, red, blue/purple, Yukon Gold, Yellow Finn, and German Butter. These varieties are often not found in grocery stores.

Preheat the oven to 325 degrees. Heat the garlic and olive oil in a large Dutch oven on the stove top. Brown the roast on all sides in the heated oil and garlic. Season the roast with salt and pepper; add the beef stock. Cover and bake for 2 hours, until the roast is tender. Add onions, carrots, and potatoes on top of the roast during the final 30 minutes.

• • •

SAUSAGE SOUFFLÉ
Loni Holley, Holley Family Farms

12 slices day-old bread, cut into 1-inch cubes	2 cups milk
	1 teaspoon dry mustard
1 pound ground sausage	1 teaspoon salt
1 cup grated sharp cheddar cheese	oregano, to taste
6 eggs, slightly beaten	marjoram, to taste

Crumble sausage into skillet; cook until lightly browned. Drain fat. Place cubed bread and sausage in greased 9"x13" pan. Top with grated cheese. In a blender, beat eggs. Add milk, dry mustard, salt, oregano, and marjoram, and blend. Pour mixture over bread in pan. Cover and refrigerate overnight.

The next morning, bake at 350 degrees for 45 to 60 minutes, until a knife inserted in the center comes out clean. Serves 6.

SUNNY DAY ORGANICS CRAFT BACON

Rebecca Stetson, Sunny Day Organics

2 ½ pounds pork belly

Spice rub

3 tablespoons kosher or other coarse,
non-iodized salt

½ cup maple sugar (or coconut or
brown sugar, but maple is the best)

2 tablespoons granulated garlic or
3 cloves garlic

1 ½ tablespoons crushed black pepper

2 teaspoons fresh or dried thyme

1 teaspoon roasted fennel seeds

1 teaspoon roasted coriander seeds

Wet ingredients

2 tablespoons whiskey, strong coffee,
or apple juice

Note: Make this bacon your own by adding red pepper, jalapeño slices, extra garlic, nutmeg, cinnamon, or whatever you fancy. My favorite woods for smoking bacon are apple and maple.

Mix together dry ingredients for the spice rub. Set aside. Rinse the pork belly and pat dry. Remove skin if still attached. Cover pork belly with wet ingredients. This allows your spice rub to adhere and absorb better. Coat the pork belly all over with the rub.

Transfer meat to a resealable 2-gallon plastic bag and refrigerate. Flip and massage the meat every day for 7 to 10 days. The bacon should be fully cured with a firm texture and no soft points. The longer you leave it, the stronger the flavor. After the last day of curing, rinse thoroughly, then pat dry.

Refrigerate the belly on a rack, uncovered, for 24 hours. Smoke the meat using a barbecue or smoker. Smoke at 200 degrees for 1 ½ hours until internal temperature reaches 150 degrees. If you don't have a smoker, you can roast the cured bacon in a 200-degree oven until internal temperature reaches 150 degrees. However, it will not have a smoked flavor.

Refrigerate or freeze to enable easy slicing. Cook as desired. To store, wrap the bacon in plastic and refrigerate up to 1 week or freeze for up to 2 months.

TOASTY PUMPKIN/WINTER SQUASH WAFFLES
Shawn Uhland

1 cup flour

1 tablespoon brown sugar

1 teaspoon baking powder

¼ teaspoon salt

1 egg, beaten

1 ¼ cups milk

⅔ cup pumpkin or winter-squash purée

4 ½ teaspoons butter, melted

⅓ cup pecans, toasted and chopped

Note: Nevada offers many varieties of winter squash. Look for butternut, buttercup, spaghetti, Carnival, acorn, Kabocha, Turban, sweet dumpling, or delicate squash. Their flavors range from slightly sweet to savory.

Preheat waffle iron. In a large bowl, combine the flour, brown sugar, baking powder, and salt. In a separate bowl, whisk together the egg, milk, pumpkin, and butter. Stir into dry ingredients until blended. Fold in pecans. Bake in waffle iron according to manufacturer's directions, until golden brown. Makes 4 waffles.

WINTER SQUASH CASSEROLE
Erica Smith

Squash casserole

6 cups cooked, mashed winter squash

½ cup butter, melted

6 eggs, beaten

½ cup brown sugar or maple syrup

½ teaspoon salt

Topping

1 cup brown sugar

½ cup butter, softened

¼ cup flour

Note: Roast and purée pumpkins and winter squash. Then freeze in pre-measured amounts. They can be defrosted and used in your favorite recipes for up to a year.

Preheat oven to 350 degrees. Grease a 9"x13" baking dish. Combine squash, butter, eggs, brown sugar or maple syrup, and salt. Mix well; spread evenly in prepared pan topping. In a small bowl, combine brown sugar, butter, and flour; mix until crumbly. Spread over squash mixture. Bake for 40 to 45 minutes, until bubbly. Serves 12.

• • •

LAMB SHANKS WITH CITRUS SOY SAUCE
Nancy Guntly-Smith, Smith Ranch

6 lamb shanks

salt and pepper, to taste

lemon pepper

garlic salt

1 cup soy sauce

1 cup lemon or lime juice

1 cup water

Note: This recipe is our family version of one from the Mendocino County Bo-peeps. For more than 40 years, our family participated in their annual Wool Growers Barbecue in Booneville. The event ended a few years ago, when the Wool Growers did not have enough young members to keep the barbecue going. It was a great time.

Preheat oven to 350 degrees. Sear the lamb shanks on stovetop or barbecue on both sides to brown. Season with salt, pepper, lemon pepper, and garlic salt. Place shanks in a roasting pan. Mix the soy sauce, lemon or lime juice, and water together, and pour over the lamb in the roaster. Cover and bake for 2 to 3 hours. Turn the shanks over several times during cooking to keep them well coated. Serves 6.

SCALLOPED SAUSAGE AND POTATO CASSEROLE
Shonet Stump

1 pound pork sausage

4 medium potatoes, peeled and thinly
  sliced (4 cups)

1 medium onion, chopped fine

4 ounces shredded cheddar cheese (1 cup)

1 ½ cups milk

¼ cup breadcrumbs

Note: Potatoes are one of the top-five commodity crops in Nevada, and Nevada ranks
18th in potato production in the United States. Nevada's climate is ideal for
potato production.

Preheat oven to 350 degrees. In skillet,
break sausage into small pieces. Brown
lightly and drain well. Place half of
the potatoes in a lightly oiled 2-quart
casserole.

Layer half of the onions over the
potatoes. Sift half of the flour over the
onions. Top with half of the sausage, then
half of the cheese.

Repeat with remaining potatoes, onions,
flour, sausage, and cheese.

Pour milk over all. Cover and bake for 50
to 60 minutes, until potatoes are tender
Uncover and sprinkle breadcrumbs on
top of casserole. Bake 10 to 15 minutes
longer, until golden. Serves 6.

SPAGHETTI SQUASH CASSEROLE
Hazel Gomes

1 medium spaghetti squash	⅛ teaspoon dried thyme
12 ounces Italian sausage	½ teaspoon salt
1 tablespoon butter	¼ teaspoon pepper
½ pound fresh mushrooms, sliced	2 medium tomatoes, chopped
1 large onion, chopped	1 cup dry bread crumbs
2 cloves garlic, minced	1 cup low-fat cottage cheese
½ teaspoon dried basil	1 cup chopped spinach
¼ teaspoon dried oregano	¼ cup grated Parmesan cheese

Note: If you have never cared for spaghetti squash, this recipe will change your mind! To make a meatless version, omit the Italian sausage and double the amount of basil, oregano, and thyme.

Preheat oven to 375 degrees. Poke holes in spaghetti squash with sharp knife to vent. Microwave squash on high for 12 minutes; set aside to cool. Brown sausage in large skillet. Drain on paper towel and set aside, discarding grease.

Melt butter in skillet. Add mushrooms, onion, garlic, basil, oregano, thyme, salt, and pepper: Sauté until onion is tender. Add tomatoes, cooking until most of the liquid has cooked down. Set aside.

Cut squash in half and discard seeds. Scoop out the squash strands with a fork. Combine squash, tomato mixture, sausage, bread crumbs, cottage cheese, and spinach.

Transfer to a greased 2-quart casserole dish. Sprinkle with Parmesan cheese. Bake, uncovered, for 40 minutes, until lightly browned on top. Serves 6.

BUTTERNUT SQUASH AND SPINACH LASAGNA
Ann Louhela

Squash

3 pounds butternut squash, quartered, peeled, and cut into ½-inch pieces (about 9 cups)

3 tablespoons olive oil

salt, to taste

Sauce

5 cups whole milk

2 tablespoons dried rosemary, crumbled

2 tablespoons garlic, minced

4 tablespoons flour

6 tablespoons butter

Assemble and bake

3 cups baby spinach, washed and chopped coarsely

9 (7"x3 ½") sheets dry no-boil lasagna pasta

1 ½ cups freshly grated Parmesan cheese (about 6 ounces)

Preheat oven to 450 degrees, and oil the bottoms of two large, shallow baking pans. In a large bowl, toss squash with olive oil and spread in one layer in pans. Roast for 10 minutes and season with salt. Stir and roast for another 10 to 15 minutes, until tender. Set aside.

While squash is roasting, in a saucepan bring milk and rosemary to a simmer. Heat mixture over low heat for 10 minutes, stirring often. Strain milk through a sieve into a large measuring cup. In a heavy saucepan, sauté garlic in butter over moderate heat until softened. Stir in flour and cook the mixture for about 3 minutes. Remove pan from heat. Gradually whisk milk into garlic mixture until smooth. Return pan to heat and simmer, stirring occasionally, for about 10 minutes, until it has thickened some. Stir in squash and salt and pepper, to taste. Sauce may be made ahead of time and chilled in refrigerator.

Reduce oven temperature to 375 degrees. Oil the bottom of a 9"x13" baking dish. Pour 1 cup sauce into baking dish (sauce will not cover bottom completely), and cover with 3 lasagna sheets. Pasta sheets should not touch each other. Spread half of remaining sauce over pasta.

Spread ⅓ of the spinach over the sauce, then sprinkle with ½ cup Parmesan. Make another layer in the same manner, ending with pasta. Sprinkle remaining ⅓ of chopped spinach over pasta sheets and sprinkle remaining ½ cup Parmesan over spinach. Cover dish tightly with foil, tenting slightly to prevent foil from touching top layer. Bake for 30 minutes. Remove foil and bake 10 minutes more, until top is bubbling and golden. Let stand 5 minutes before serving. Serves 12.

ONION PIE (CALZONE)
Karen Foster, Hidden Valley Honey

Crust

2 cups flour

2 teaspoons baking powder

½ cup olive oil

¼ cup milk

½ teaspoon salt

Filling

2 tablespoons olive oil

5 bunches green onions, chopped
(approximately 5 cups)

2 large yellow onions, sliced in half rings
¼-inch thick (approximately 4 to 5 cups)

3 eggs, beaten with 2 tablespoons water

1 cup shredded mozzarella cheese

1 cup grated Parmesan cheese

1 tablespoon sugar

½ teaspoon salt

½ teaspoon pepper

Note: My grandmother was a wonderful cook, and this is one of her recipes that we managed to preserve in writing before she passed on. She always called it just simply "calzone."

Crust

Mix together all crust ingredients with a pastry cutter or two forks until coarse crumbs form. You can also use a food processor. Let rest for 15 minutes. Divide dough between two 9-inch pie pans and press evenly on bottom and up sides of each. Add a little more milk if mixture is too crumbly. Set aside and prepare filling.

Filling

Preheat oven to 400 degrees. Heat olive oil in large, non-stick sauté pan on medium heat. Add green onions and yellow onions and cook until translucent, 5 to 10 minutes.

Remove from heat and transfer to a large bowl. Add the eggs and water, cheeses, sugar, salt, and pepper to onions. Mix well. If mixture seems dry, add one extra egg.

Divide mixture in half, and fill the 2 crust-lined pie plates. Bake pies until set and lightly browned, about 25 minutes. Do not overcook. Let cool slightly, then serve warm for brunch, lunch, or dinner. Makes 2 pies. Serves 12.

BUTTERNUT SQUASH MAC AND CHEESE
Desiree Vickrey

8 ounces pasta (macaroni, rotini, penne, or shells)

2 cups cooked butternut squash, puréed

2 cups yogurt

½ cup milk

1 teaspoon fresh thyme leaves
(or ½ teaspoon dried thyme)

1 teaspoon Dijon mustard

½ teaspoon salt

½ teaspoon black pepper, freshly ground

1 teaspoon garlic powder

12 ounces shredded sharp cheddar cheese

4 tablespoons breadcrumbs

Note: Nevada farmers grow several varieties of squash. In the summer, look for trombone, yellow crookneck, patty pan, green and yellow zucchini, and two round squash referred to as "one ball" (yellow in color) and "eight ball" (dark green in color).

Preheat oven to 350 degrees. Cook the pasta until al dente, according to package instructions. Drain the water and set the pasta aside.

Combine squash, yogurt, milk, thyme, mustard, salt, pepper, garlic powder, and cheddar cheese. Mix well. Add the pasta to the cheese-squash mixture. Place in a greased 2-quart baking dish. Sprinkle the top with breadcrumbs. Bake for 30 to 40 minutes, until bubbly and breadcrumbs are browned. Serves 6.

PASTA WITH SAVORY BUTTERNUT SQUASH SAUCE
Heidi Parker

1 butternut squash, medium sized

3 to 5 tablespoons olive oil

salt and pepper, to taste

4 to 6 cloves garlic, roasted

one bunch (fist-full) fresh sage,
chopped fine

1 to 2 cups vegetable broth

1 pound cooked pasta of your choice—
linguine or rigatoni works great

handful of spinach, chopped (optional)

Parmigiana Reggiano cheese, grated
(or Parmesan) as topping

Note: I once read that this is a seasonal dish found throughout Italy. I have adapted it to utilize the fall bounty of Northern Nevada. It is flavorful, filling, and makes your house smell delicious! If there is any left, it reheats great for lunch the next day. The sauce can also be served over rice or quinoa instead of pasta.

Preheat oven to 375 degrees. Cut squash in half and scoop out the seeds. Brush the squash halves with olive oil, and lightly sprinkle with salt and fresh-ground pepper. Place cut sides down on baking sheet. Roast about 30 minutes, until slightly soft. Remove from oven, and cool slightly. Peel and chop into large chunks.

Heat remaining olive oil in deep sauté pan on medium heat. Sauté garlic until lightly browned and softened. Add chopped sage. Add squash and sauté on medium-low heat until it turns a darker color and is cooked through, about 10 to 15 minutes.

Add 1 cup vegetable broth and cook until squash starts to resemble chunky sauce. Add more broth for thinner sauce or to a consistency of your liking. Add salt or pepper, to taste. Simmer on low until pasta is ready. For additional color, add a handful of chopped spinach.

Cook pasta according to package directions until al dente. Drain. Mix the pasta with the squash sauce in the pasta pot. Serve with a bowl of grated cheese on the side for garnish and crusty bread for dipping. Serves 6.

WAIKIKI MEATBALLS
Shonet Stump

Meatballs	Sauce
1 ½ pounds ground beef	2 tablespoons cornstarch
⅔ cup saltine-cracker crumbs	½ cup brown sugar, packed
⅓ cup white onion, minced	1 (13.5-ounce) can pineapple chunks, drained, with syrup reserved
1 egg	
¼ cup milk	¼ cup apple-cider vinegar
1 ½ teaspoons salt	1 tablespoon soy sauce
½ teaspoon ground ginger	1 bell pepper, cut into one-inch pieces

Note: About 780,000 pounds of milk are produced annually in Northern Nevada dairies.

In a large bowl, mix thoroughly the ground beef, cracker crumbs, onion, egg, milk, salt, and ginger until completely combined. Shape rounded tablespoonfuls of mixture into balls.

Heat a large nonstick skillet to medium heat. Brown meatballs until done, about 15 minutes, working in batches if necessary. Place meatballs on a cooking sheet and keep warm. Pour fat from skillet and discard.

In a second mixing bowl, mix cornstarch and brown sugar. Add reserved pineapple syrup, vinegar, and soy sauce and stir until smooth.

Pour into the same skillet used to cook the meatballs. Cook over medium heat, stirring constantly, until mixture thickens and boils.

Let boil for one minute, stirring constantly. Add cooked meatballs, pineapple chunks, and bell pepper to skillet. Stir and heat through. If desired, warm in a slow cooker for party appetizers or serve as a main course over rice. Makes 6 servings.

CHICKEN CACCIATORE
Sue Kennedy, Kennedy Ranch

Whole chicken, cut up into 10 pieces (wings, breasts, thighs, legs). Cut breasts in half to make four breast pieces, and save the neck, back, and wing tips for making soup stock another day.

2 teaspoons salt

1 teaspoon pepper

½ cup all-purpose flour

3 tablespoons olive oil

1 large red bell pepper, chopped

1 large onion, chopped

1 head garlic, cloves separated and peeled, put through a garlic press

¾ cup dry white wine

1 quart jar canned tomatoes (or a 28-ounce can stewed tomatoes)

3 tablespoons drained capers

1 ½ tablespoons chopped fresh oregano, or ½ teaspoon dried oregano leaves

¼ cup fresh basil leaves

Pat chicken pieces dry. If you have time, let them sit in the refrigerator uncovered for a couple of hours before you start cooking to let the skin dry (saves splattering).

Mix flour, salt, and pepper in a brown paper bag. Shake each chicken piece in bag, individually, to lightly coat. Put in a single layer on a plate.

Heat olive oil in Dutch oven until hot. Put pieces in pot a few at a time, without crowding, and brown both sides. Do multiple batches if you need to. Watch the temperature; don't let it burn. Transfer chicken to a different plate and set aside. Pour off all but about 1 tablespoon of the fat. Add bell pepper, onion, and garlic to pot. Sauté until onion is tender. Add wine and simmer until reduced by half.

Add chicken, tomatoes, capers, oregano, and basil to Dutch oven. Cover and cook on the stovetop on low heat for about 30 minutes or until chicken is thoroughly cooked. Served 4.

MOZZARELLA POTATO SOUFFLÉ
Carolyn Turner

2 large russet potatoes

2 tablespoons unsalted butter

2 tablespoons all-purpose flour

½ cup reduced-fat or whole milk

¼ teaspoon salt

pinch red pepper flakes (optional)

½ cup shredded mozzarella cheese

2 tablespoons grated Parmesan cheese

2 large eggs, separated

Note: Be sure to serve the skins right away, because the soufflé filling won't stay puffed. I love mozzarella cheese and russet potatoes, so I decided to combine the two for a great meal. My whole family loves it.

Preheat oven to 400 degrees. Lightly grease a baking sheet. Bake potatoes until flesh can easily be pierced with a fork, about 45 minutes to 1 hour. Let sit until cool enough to handle.

Cut each potato in half lengthwise, and using a spoon, hollow out center, leaving a shell about ⅛-inch thick. Discard potato flesh or reserve for another recipe. Place shells, hollow side up, on prepared baking sheet.

Place potatoes in oven to keep warm while assembling soufflé base. In a small saucepan, melt butter over medium-low heat. Add flour and stir with a wooden spoon to form a light roux, about 2 minutes. Gradually add milk and whisk constantly until thick, 4 to 5 minutes.

Remove from heat and add salt, cheeses, and red pepper flakes (if using), and whisk to combine. Let sit 2 minutes, then add egg yolks and whisk.

In a mixing bowl with whisk attachment, whip the 2 egg whites to slightly stiff peaks. Fold into cheese mixture in 3 additions.

Using a pastry bag or small spoon, fill potato skins with soufflé mixture. Bake without opening oven door for 10 minutes, then reduce temperature to 375 degrees. Continue baking until puffed and golden brown, 15 to 20 minutes. Serves 4.

NUTTY AND SPICY PUMPKIN BREAD
Jana Vanderhaar

4 cups flour (can be a mix of white, whole-wheat, wheat germ, or wheat-free flour)

1 cup cane or coconut sugar

2 teaspoons baking soda

2 teaspoons salt

2 teaspoons cinnamon

1 teaspoon nutmeg

1 teaspoon cloves

1 teaspoon ginger

2 ½ cups pumpkin or winter squash, cooked and puréed

4 eggs, lightly beaten

½ cup sunflower oil

½ cup chopped nuts (pecans, walnuts, or almonds)

1 cup raisins

Note: Cooking pumpkins go beyond the traditional small orange sugar pie pumpkins. Look for white, red kuri, blue hoddaiko, winter luxury, and long pie. Not only do they taste wonderful, they also make beautiful centerpieces.

Preheat oven to 350 degrees. Oil two 5"x9" loaf pans. In large bowl, mix flour, sugar, baking soda, salt, cinnamon, nutmeg, cloves, and ginger. Set aside.

In a medium bowl, mix pumpkin or squash, eggs, oil, nuts, and raisins. Add to the dry ingredients and mix until just moistened. Don't overmix. Pour batter into prepared pans.

Bake for approximately 55 minutes, until toothpick inserted in center of loaves comes out clean. Cool in pans on wire rack for 10 minutes.

Loosen edges and turn loaves out to cool completely before serving. This recipe can also be used for muffins in muffin tins—bake muffins for 10 to 15 minutes. Makes 2 loaves.

HONEY APPLESAUCE CAKE
Debbie Gilmore, Hall's Honey

½ cup butter, room temperature

¾ cup honey

½ cup applesauce, warmed

1 ½ cups flour

¼ teaspoon ground cloves

¼ teaspoon ground ginger

½ teaspoon cinnamon

1 cup raisins

½ cup chopped walnuts or pecans

1 teaspoon baking soda

1 tablespoon hot water

Note: This is from my grandmother's recipe collection. The honey and raisins make for a sweet cake, and it doesn't need any frosting. I sometimes use half whole-wheat and half white flour in the recipe.

Preheat oven to 350 degrees. Grease and flour an 8"x8" cake pan. In a large mixing bowl, cream butter with honey. Add warmed applesauce and mix well.

In separate bowl, mix flour, cloves, ginger, cinnamon, raisins, and nuts. Mix dry ingredients into honey mixture.

Dissolve baking soda into 1 tablespoon hot water and mix quickly into batter. Pour batter into baking pan. Bake for 35 to 40 minutes, until toothpick inserted in center comes out clean. Serve warm or cold. Serves 16.

HONEY NUT BROWNIES
Debbie Gilmore, Hall's Honey

---

2 ounces unsweetened chocolate, melted

2 eggs

½ cup sugar

½ cup honey

⅓ cup butter, melted

½ cup flour

¼ teaspoon baking powder

¼ teaspoon salt

1 cup chopped walnuts

Note: Due to our dry climate, Nevada honey is thicker than honey produced in other regions because it has a lower moisture content.

Preheat oven to 350 degrees. Line an 8"x8" pan with parchment paper to prevent sticking. Microwave chocolate in microwaveable bowl on high for 30 seconds and stir. Microwave 30 seconds more and stir again. Continue heating and stirring in 10-second increments until completely melted.

In a large bowl, beat eggs and sugar until thick. Add honey and blend. Add butter to melted chocolate and add to egg mixture.

Combine flour, baking powder, and salt. Blend thoroughly with egg mixture. Add nuts and stir to combine. Pour into prepared pan.

Bake for 35 to 40 minutes, until toothpick in center comes out clean. Cool the brownies. Invert the pan; remove parchment paper and cut the brownies into squares. Serves 16.

PUMPKIN PEANUT BUTTER FUDGE
Virginia Gibbs

3 cups white sugar	1 teaspoon pumpkin-pie spice
1 cup whole milk	1 ½ teaspoons vanilla extract
3 tablespoons light corn syrup	¼ cup butter
1 cup homemade pumpkin purée	⅓ cup natural peanut butter
¼ teaspoon salt	½ cup chopped walnuts (optional)

Note: This is one of my favorite recipes for Christmas candy.

Butter or grease an 8"x8" pan. In a 3-quart saucepan, mix together sugar, milk, corn syrup, pumpkin, and salt. Bring to a boil over high heat, stirring constantly. Reduce heat to medium and continue boiling. Do not stir.

When mixture registers 232 degrees on a candy thermometer, or forms a soft ball when dropped into cold water, remove pan from heat. Stir in pumpkin pie spice, vanilla, butter, peanut butter, and nuts. Cool to lukewarm (110 degrees on a candy thermometer).

Beat mixture until it is very thick and loses some of its gloss. Quickly pour into pan. When firm, cut into 36 squares.

WINTER SQUASH SQUARES
Rae Vallem

Squares

2 cups all-purpose flour

2 cups sugar

2 teaspoons baking powder

1 teaspoon baking soda

½ teaspoon cinnamon

⅛ teaspoon salt

4 eggs, beaten

2 cups cooked winter squash, puréed

1 cup oil

Frosting

1 (3-ounce) package cream cheese, softened

2 cups confectioners sugar

1 teaspoon vanilla extract

6 tablespoons butter, softened

1 tablespoon milk

Note: Puréed pumpkin can be substituted for the winter squash.

Squares

Preheat oven to 350 degrees. Oil a 10"x15"x1" baking pan. In a large bowl, combine flour, sugar, baking powder, baking soda, cinnamon, and salt.

Stir in eggs, squash, and oil; mix well. Spread into prepared pan. Bake for 25 to 30 minutes, until a toothpick inserted in the center comes out clean. Cool on a wire rack.

Frosting

In a medium bowl, beat together cream cheese, sugar, vanilla, and butter. Add milk and stir until smooth. Frost the cooled cake. Cut into squares. Yields 4 dozen.

HONEY RICE CUSTARD
Debbie Gilmore, Hall's Honey

2 eggs	1 cup cooked rice
½ cup honey	nutmeg, to taste
¼ teaspoon salt	cinnamon, to taste
½ teaspoon vanilla	brown sugar (optional)
2 cups milk	

Note: This old family recipe is especially delicious sprinkled with brown sugar.

Preheat oven to 350 degrees. Grease an 8-inch square baking pan. Beat eggs slightly. Add honey, salt, and vanilla. Stir well. Add the milk and cooked rice and pour into prepared pan. Sprinkle with nutmeg and cinnamon, to taste.

Bake for 40 minutes, until knife inserted in center comes out clean. Sprinkle lightly with brown sugar (if using). Cool before serving. Serves 9.

• • •

CHOCOLATE HONEY LOAF
Debbie Gilmore, Hall's Honey

1 egg	½ teaspoon salt
2 tablespoons butter	2 ½ teaspoons baking powder
1 cup honey	½ teaspoon baking soda
¾ cup orange juice	¾ cup chopped walnuts
1 tablespoon orange rind	1 (12-ounce) package semi-sweet
2 ¾ cups flour	chocolate chips, divided

Preheat oven to 350 degrees. Grease two 4"x8 ½" loaf pans. Cream egg, butter, and honey. Mix orange juice and orange rind into the honey mixture. Beat in the flour, salt, baking powder, and baking soda. Stir in nuts and 1 cup of the chocolate chips. Pour into prepared loaf pans. Sprinkle the rest of the chocolate chips on top and bake for 30 to 40 minutes, until toothpick inserted in center comes out clean. Makes 2 loaves.

THREE-GINGER HOLI-DAZE COOKIES
Virginia Johnson, Custom Gardens Organic Farm

1 cup sugar

¼ cup butter, room temperature

1 to 2 tablespoons grated fresh baby
ginger root

2 tablespoons molasses

1 whole egg

1 ½ cups all-purpose flour

1 teaspoon baking soda

½ teaspoon ground ginger

2 tablespoons finely chopped
crystallized ginger

½ cup finely chopped dates, dried currants,
or finely chopped nuts (optional)

½ cup sugar for rolling cookie-dough balls

Note: We make these cookies with fresh baby ginger root grown at our farm.

In a large mixing bowl, combine 1 cup sugar, butter, ginger root, molasses, and the egg. Mix well. Stir in flour, baking soda, and ground ginger. Add crystallized ginger and dates, nuts, or currants (optional). Cover and refrigerate for at least 2 hours.

Preheat oven to 350 degrees. Spray cookie sheet with nonstick cooking spray or use parchment paper. Shape dough into 1-inch balls. Roll each one in ½ cup sugar and place on cookie sheet. Flatten slightly with bottom of glass. Bake 11 to 14 minutes, until only a small indentation remains when touched. Cookies will be soft. Remove from cookie sheet and cool on a wire rack. Makes 24 cookies.

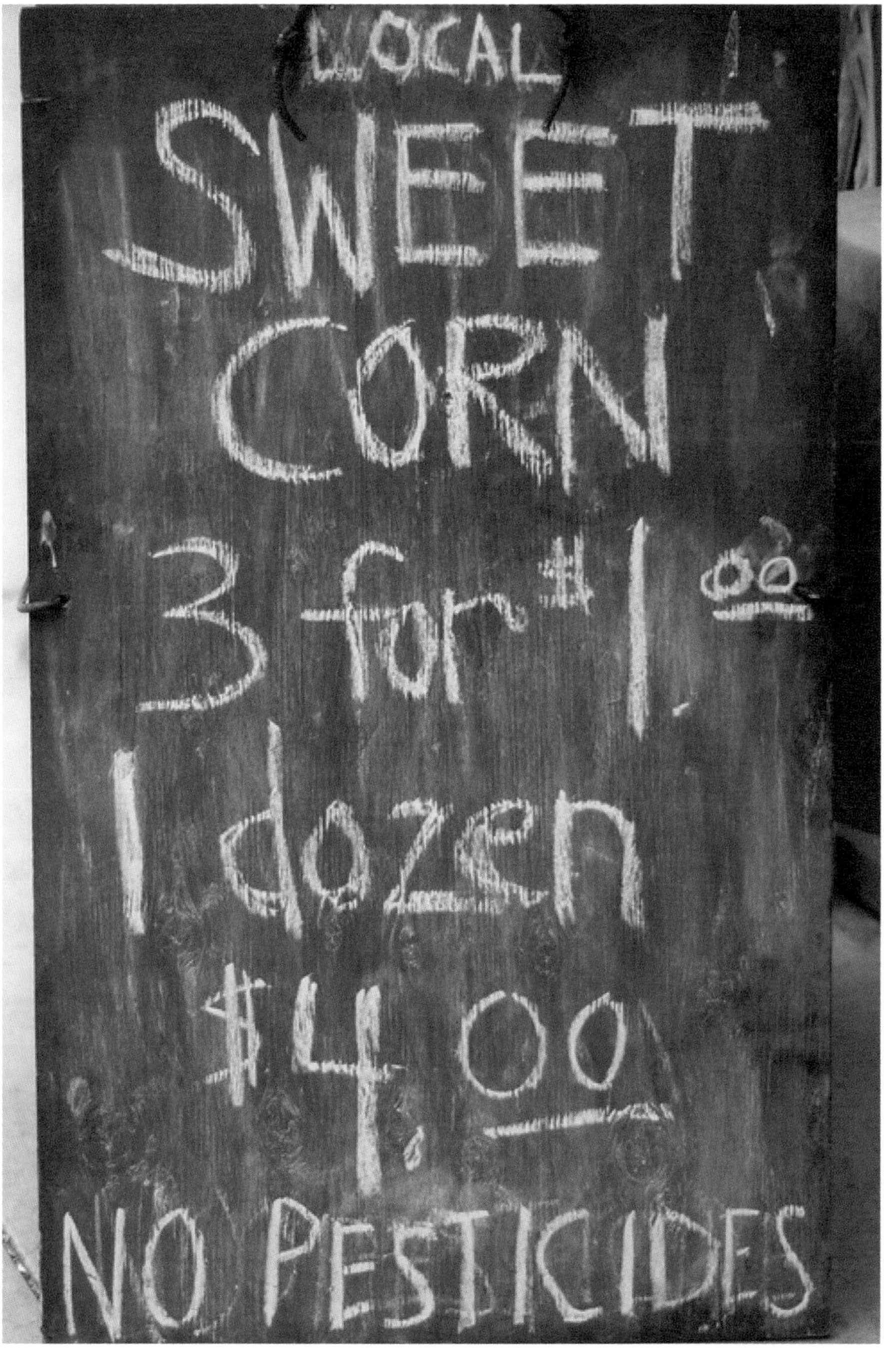
LOCAL
SWEET
CORN
3 for $1.00
1 dozen
$4.00
NO PESTICIDES

ACKNOWLEDGMENTS

Writing a cookbook is a monumental task, from collecting, testing, and editing recipes to taking professional photographs and creating graphic design. Two years in the making, we collected recipes from chefs, home cooks, farmers, and ranchers. The one requirement was that recipes contain ingredients grown or produced in Nevada. We tested and tasted almost 200 recipes and compiled our favorites into this book, more than 150 recipes to take you through the seasons.

Cookbook Co-Editor Johnathan L. Wright

Johnathan L. Wright, food and drink editor of RGJ Media, was our trusted advisor, keeping the book on track for quality and content and patiently guiding a group of naïve amateurs through the process of creating a professional cookbook. He set standards for recipe ingredients (no canned soup!), and thank goodness, he insisted that we test every recipe. In a yearlong Home Means Delicious campaign in the *Reno Gazette-Journal* and on RGJ.com, Johnathan highlighted Nevada's farms, ranches, and foods in a series of articles complete with recipes. Under Johnathan's watchful eye, *Nevada Grown: A Year in Local Food* was born.

Recipe Editor Laura Longero Holman

Laura earned our admiration as recipe editor. For months, she tested and rewrote recipes, then cooked and baked them to picture-perfect perfection. All of the beautiful recipe photos came from Laura's kitchen. In the midst of creating this book, Laura gave birth to a beautiful baby daughter, Aurelia, who spent the first three months of her life in the kitchen with Mom creating *Nevada Grown: A Year in Local Food*. Lucky Aurelia!

Underwriter Western Nevada College Specialty Crop Institute

Project director Ann Louhela and staff provided the administrative and financial support to make the cookbook a reality. From matching lost recipes to their contributors to submitting the final copy to the publisher, WNC Specialty Crop Institute provided the foundation for the project to grow.

Loyal Recipe Testers

With almost 200 recipes to test, our recipe editor needed help. We thank the adventurous volunteers who discovered gastric treasures, filled in the missing ingredients and correct cooking times, and deciphered great-grandma's fourth-generation recipe. They shared their mishaps and successes with merriment as their kitchens filled with the sights and smells of NevadaGrown home cookin'.

Recipe Contributors

Your recipes and passion for good food are truly the soul of this cookbook!

Recipe Index

Contributor Index

***These farms, ranches, markets, restaurants, animals, produce,and landscapes
can be found in:**

Boulder City, Caliente, Carson City, Dayton, Fallon, Gardnerville, Las Vegas, Minden,
Reno, Silver Springs, Smith Valley, Sparks, Wellington, Yerington

NOTES

NOTES